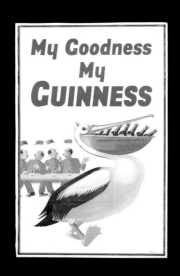

My Goodness
My
GUINNESS

The Book of Guinness Advertising

Jim Davies

GUINNESS PUBLISHING

British Library Cataloguing in Publication Data

A catalogue record for this book is available from the British Library

ISBN 0-85112-067-9

Managing Editor

Mark Fletcher

Editors

Sara Harper

Sarah Taylor

Researcher

Mari Takayanagi

Proofreader

Ian Julier

Indexer

Kathie Gill

Publishing Director

Ian Castello-Cortes

Design

Peter Jackson

Design Assistants

Keith Jackson

Adam Kelsey

Cover

Lolli Aboutboul Design

Photography

Robert Clifford

Production

Patricia Langton

Chris Lingard

Colour Origination

Dot Gradations Ltd

Printing and Binding

Butler & Tanner Ltd

Author

Jim Davies is a journalist, copywriter and internet editor. He has written for specialist design and advertising titles such as *Eye, Design* and *Campaign*, as well as for the *Guardian*, the *Independent*, the *Daily Telegraph* and the *Sunday Times Magazine*. He was on the 1997 D&AD jury for Interactive Design and the BAFTA jury for Graphic Design.

Contents

Artwork 1953

Agency SH Benson

Artist J Gilroy

Preface

The Book of Guinness Advertising is a celebration of an extraordinary brand. It is hard to think of a beer which over two centuries has been held in such affection and has, to many around the world, come to symbolise a way of life. This is due in no small part to the advertising which, arguably without equals, has maintained a quality and character so high that it has attracted its own brand loyalty.

It gives me particular pleasure that this book is being published in the year that we at Guinness celebrate the centenary of John Gilroy's birth. Gilroy, with his menagerie of characters which included the ubiquitous toucan, was the artist who in many people's minds came to define an essential image of Guinness. His work is on display in many of the c1800 Irish pubs around the world adding immensely to the Guinness experience.

In his day, Gilroy was an innovator. As you turn the pages of this book this is the characteristic which stands out: the extraordinary creativity and originality of the artists, illustrators, photographers,

graphic designers and film makers who kept the Guinness brand at the forefront of advertising in every decade since the 1920s. From the revival of the toucan in the 1970s, through the Genius campaigns of the 1980s, and including the "Black and White" campaigns of the 1990s Guinness advertising has captured the zeitgeist of its target markets.

Guinness advertising continues to do so as we write. The images may change from year to year, from market to market. One constant, however, remains and that is the complex qualities that make a glass of Guinness so special. It is in that experience that the creativity in these pages ultimately draws its inspiration.

Colin Storm
Chief Executive
Guinness
Park Royal
London

Introduction

The first national advertisement for *Guinness* stout appeared in several British daily newspapers on February 7, 1929. Self-important, it was an inauspicious beginning for a brand that over the next 70 years was to become associated with highly accomplished, often inspired advertising campaigns. But Guinness' first press advertisement did have one important redeeming feature: it introduced the famous sign-off line, "Guinness is good for you", which struck a chord with the British public and quickly passed into the vernacular. Despite being discarded over 30 years ago, when the advertising regulatory bodies began flexing their muscles, it remains a familiar slogan, testament to its deep emotional resonance.

Press advertisement 7 February 1929

Agency SH Benson

Guinness' first British press advertisement
appeared in several national newspapers.

Poster 1934

Agency SH Benson

Artist J Gilroy

The "Man with the girder" became such an institution
that in the 1970s it was parodied by Heineken.

It is impossible to compare directly the intuitive,
often brilliant press advertisements and posters of the
1930s, 1940s and 1950s with the sophisticated, multi-
faceted advertising campaigns of the 1970s onwards.
John Gilroy's "girder" poster (1934) may have a certain
timeless quality, but you can hardly judge it by the
same criteria as a commercial from Ogilvy & Mather's
esoteric "Man with the Guinness" campaign
(1987–1995). By the same token, it is a quite fruitless

exercise attempting to measure the effectiveness of a
1990s web site against a 1930s pub show card.

Public attitudes and perceptions have changed
dramatically since Guinness first became involved in
advertising, as have marketing techniques, media
channels and the day-to-day working vocabulary
employed by advertisers. Bombarded with an
estimated 13,000 commercial messages per day

A GOOD EVENING'S ENTERTAINMENT.

Poster 1981

Agency J Walter Thompson
Photographer M Thomson

J Walter Thompson successfully took *Guinness* advertising into the television era.

(including advertisements, logos and various corporate plugs), the modern consumer has evolved into an expert decoder, capable of understanding even the most complex sponsored messages.

Since the 1960s, television has established itself as easily the most dominant advertising medium, but for how much longer? Satellite, cable and now digital television have spawned a host of new specialist channels, fragmenting a once guaranteed audience for commercials. Advertisers may be able to target consumers more accurately by creating advertisements tailored to specific audiences and placing them with relevant broadcasters, but the days when a major new advertising campaign was a "shared cultural experience" are over. Meanwhile, the full impact of the Internet and interactive television have still yet to be felt.

Whatever the dominant medium of the age, *Guinness* advertising has strived to exploit it fully. In 1995, for instance, at least 100,000 people downloaded a *Guinness* screensaver from the Internet (www.guinness.ie). But if the tone, attitude and method of delivery has varied over the decades, the core message has remained consistent; *Guinness* is a unique, high-quality product with a strong personality.

The advertising has maintained a surprisingly consistent standard. In a leader column in the British advertising industry's weekly mouthpiece *Campaign*, editor Stefano Hatfield wrote: "Guinness is not just an advertising icon, in Britain it is *the* advertising icon. Any student of advertising would have to conclude that it has been the most consistently excellent advertiser of the century. Despite the inevitable highs and lows... it is arguably the brand of the century."

There is no doubt that the drink's physical manifestation has been critical to its long-standing popularity; indeed, its distinctive black body and creamy white head has often been likened to "a logo in a glass". In his seminal treatise on advertising psychology, *The Strategy of Desire* (1960), the American social scientist Ernest Dichter writes, "that after all the millions of dollars that [the advertiser] may have expended in advertising and public relations and merchandising, the real measure of his success is the creation of a personality and a uniqueness for his brand and product. If he has failed to establish such a uniqueness, then indeed, his advertising program has failed." In terms of its marketing strategy, then, *Guinness* has enjoyed a distinct advantage over most beers; until the recent explosion of stout brands on the market (some genuine, others contrived), it has stood defiantly alone, palpably different from its bitter and lager rivals, a point that its advertising has consistently emphasised. *Guinness* is a true one-off, so quite sensibly, its defining values have remained central to its advertising strategy.

At the turn of the century Samuel (SH) Benson, founder of the advertising agency that bore his name (which went on to handle the Guinness account for 41 years), wrote that his main criteria for accepting an advertising commission was that the product should be socially acceptable and available at a reasonable price. This sentiment was ahead of its time, hinting at what would later become defined as "brand values" and "product integrity", but more importantly, he recognised that advertising – no matter how inventive – can never be a substitute for shoddy goods. The product has always proudly taken centre stage in *Guinness* advertising; its innate characteristics providing the basis for a succession of diverse, imaginative campaigns.

Primarily because of its Irish heritage, *Guinness* stout has occupied a slightly unusual position within the

British brewing industry which has influenced its advertising strategy. Until the Guinness Park Royal Brewery was established in London in 1936, all *Guinness* stout was imported to Great Britain from Dublin. Traditionally, many pubs in Britain were "tied houses", that is, owned by a particular brewery who, naturally enough, saw them as guaranteed purchase points for their own beers. Though Guinness didn't own a single pub itself, the stout had managed to infiltrate virtually every pub in the country, which meant that it could legitimately claim to be the most popular beer in the land – and did. But this arrangement was precarious, as it meant that the availability of *Guinness* in public houses was always reliant on the level of customer demand. Therefore, a prime task of *Guinness* advertising was to ensure that this demand continued to justify stocking it in these "tied houses".

Over a period of nearly 70 years, the challenging task of advertising *Guinness* has been carried out by five agencies in Britain: SH Benson (1927–1969); J Walter Thompson (1969–1982); Allen, Brady & Marsh (1982–1984), Ogilvy & Mather (1984–1998) and the incumbent Abbott Mead Vickers BBDO (1998–). Each has managed to distil and broadcast the brand's message using the grammar contemporary to advertising; but the similarities more or less end there.

Bensons is best remembered for the virtuoso poster artistry of John Gilroy. In *Ogilvy On Advertising*, David Ogilvy, one of the most influential figures in modern advertising, maintains that: "[Gilroy's posters] made Guinness part of the warp and woof of English life, and have never been excelled – anywhere." Gilroy's characters certainly had immense populist appeal, and his synthesis of skilled draughtsmanship and gentle humour elevated Bensons' early "My goodness, my Guinness" and "Guinness for Strength" poster campaigns, in particular, to classic status. The ostrich swallowing the glass of *Guinness* whole, the sea lion making off with the glass of *Guinness* on its

Poster 1936

Agency SH Benson
Artist J Gilroy

Gilroy's ostrich poster
ranks among the most
enduring advertising
images of all time.

nose and the jaunty, flat-capped workman casually
carrying the impossibly large girder remain three of
the most potent advertising images ever created. By
the time World War II broke out, Bensons' poster
campaign had achieved such high recognition and
momentum that it could easily be adapted to support
the war effort and the post-war productivity drive.
But there was more to Bensons than Gilroy. Dorothy L
Sayers, later to become famous for her crime fiction,
was part of Bensons' writing team and credited with
having conceived the *Guinness* toucan, which was
used on several Gilroy posters, countless pieces of
merchandise, and later revived for a 1970s J Walter
Thompson campaign. Abram Games and Tom

Eckersley, two of the country's leading graphic
designers of the post-war era, contributed poster
designs as Guinness introduced a more incisive visual
aesthetic during the late 1950s and early 1960s. A host
of top illustrators and cartoonists – HM Bateman,
Fougasse, Antony Groves-Raines and Bruce Hobbs
among them – produced press advertisements,
elaborate giveaway books and countless pieces of
collectable promotional material.

Staff changes at Bensons and the fact that the agency
never fully came to terms with the demands of
television advertising saw Guinness switch its
advertising account to the American-owned J Walter

Lovely day for a GUINNESS

Poster 1955

Agency SH Benson
Artist J Gilroy

The toucan was repeatedly used in *Guinness* campaigns from the 1950s through to the late 1970s.

Thompson in 1969. It was a tough decision, but relations with Bensons had become decidedly uneasy. As Alan Wood, Advertising Director of Guinness at the time noted: "Bensons were losing accounts, morale was low and it was clear that the longer we waited, the more damaging the blow would be if we did leave... From the start, J Walter Thompson did some marvellous work and they had the good sense and the confidence to resist the temptation to stand Guinness advertising on its head just to rub in that Guinness had changed agencies for the first time."

J Walter Thompson, fronted by creative director Jeremy Bullmore, took *Guinness* advertising into a new era.

The agency's poster work was characterised by impeccable photography and droll puns – some less painful than others. "Tall, dark and have some" and "A little dark refreshment" were typical of the genre. Press advertisements often took the form of intricate send-ups such as the "Foreigner's guide to Guinness", which featured a cut-out coupon with the words, "Give me a Guinness" printed on it and the instructions, "If in doubt about your command of English, cut this out and simply hand it to the barman". Another stylish press campaign targeted women drinkers, using the leading fashion photographers of the day to give *Guinness* a glamorous, even sexy, image.

Are you afraid of the dark?

Poster 1972

Agency J Walter Thompson

In the 1970s, *Guinness* advertising strove to challenge the perceptions of the typical beer drinker.

More significantly, J Walter Thompson established Guinness as a major force in the television commercials arena. Many of these films were well-observed, sharply written pub-based scenarios, usually including a gag, but always putting across a salient point about *Guinness*. High-profile directors who worked on *Guinness* commercials during this period included Terence Donovan, Lindsay Anderson and Karel Reiss. The *Guinness* toucan reappeared, to become the star of a popular long-running series of commercials, as well as press and poster work.

Though they were showered with international creative awards, J Walter Thompson's advertising campaigns eventually became a victim of their own success. Sales of *Guinness* were in decline, and while consumers claimed they adored the advertising, it appeared to bear little or no correlation to their drinking patterns. Extreme measures were required, so Guinness turned to the agency Allen, Brady & Marsh, which was renowned for its aggressive, no-frills, results-driven approach to advertising.

In 1983, Allen, Brady & Marsh unveiled its £7 million "Guinnless" campaign, which had been heralded as, "the most researched, thoroughly thought-out campaign in the history of British advertising". The first poster showed an empty glass together with the legend "Guinnless isn't good for you", a reversal of Bensons' original slogan; elaborations on this basic idea were subsequently extended across all media. Seven television commercials were aired over the period 1983–8, all focusing on the problems of the Guinnless, people who had been without a *Guinness* for too long, and The Friends of the Guinnless, an organisation to help them with this problem. Recall was phenomenal, but not always positive. Guinness sales stabilised, even increased slightly. Allen, Brady & Marsh had achieved its objectives, but nevertheless lost the account.

Ogilvy & Mather was selected to take *Guinness'* advertising into the next, longer-term phase. It too had conducted an extensive research programme before launching the spectacular "Pure Genius" campaign of 1985. The agency had developed a two-pronged strategy: one strand promoting the inherent values of the product itself, the other homing in on the consumer, suggesting the type of person likely to drink *Guinness*. At first, two pairs of very different

Bus side 1987

Agency Ogilvy & Mather

The "Pure Genius" campaign ran from 1985 until 1996 when it was replaced with the "Black and White" campaign.

Poster 1996

Agency Ogilvy & Mather

This poster was used on the London Underground. Guinness have a long tradition of clever, site-specific advertisements.

commercials were aired to address these aspects of the brand, but in 1987 they were both distilled into the long-running "Man with the Guinness" campaign, featuring the Dutch-born actor Rutger Hauer.

By the mid-1990s, several major beer brands were using a similar format to the "Man with the Guinness" commercials, using an enigmatic spokesman to articulate and personify the inner qualities of their product, in a quirky, lateral way. Guinness therefore decided to change tack, and after a brief hiatus – in which "Anticipation", a hugely successful commercial by Guinness' Irish advertising agency Arks, was aired – introduced the "Black and White" campaign.

The edgy, slightly controversial "Black and White" campaign couldn't have been further removed from the cosy familiarity of Gilroy's posters, but nevertheless it continued the long tradition of advertising excellence fostered by Guinness. During that period, the advertising industry has matured and become markedly more complex, witnessing many

exciting breakthrough campaigns along the way. It remains to be seen what the newly appointed guardian of *Guinness* advertising, Abbott Mead Vickers BBDO, will achieve for the brand, but its recent portfolio of work is outstanding.

"You can be sure of Shell" and the Bisto kids from the 1930s; Abram Games' Ministry of Information posters from the 1940s; Bill Bernbach's seminal Volkswagen press campaign from the 1960s; Collett Dickenson Pearce's surreal Benson & Hedges posters in the 1970s; Bartle Bogle Hegarty's work for Levi's jeans during the 1980s; Wieden and Kennedy's work for Nike in the 1990s: there are others worthy of note, but few would argue that the above rank among some of the most powerful examples of advertising of their time. With the notable exception of *Guinness*, however, it is more difficult to cite a major brand which has managed to sustain such excellent advertising in a range of media over five decades. This book is a celebration of a unique achievement by a unique brand. □

Guinness is good for you

Market research has not always been an exacting science. Focus groups,

blind tastings, one-way mirrors, quantitative, qualitative and motivational

analysis were all some way off when SH Benson was appointed as

Guinness' first advertising agency back in 1927. Oswald Greene, a director

and copywriter at the agency and Bobby Bevan, a junior copywriter, who

was later to become Chairman and Managing Director, set about gathering

background information and ammunition for the inaugural *Guinness*

advertising campaign. The first stop was an extensive tour around the

Guinness Brewery in Dublin. Every nuance and peculiarity of stout brewing

was thoroughly examined as a possible springboard for creative ideas.

Even now, the factory visit is still a considered a legitimate and fruitful

starting point for many contemporary campaigns.

Poster 1932

Agency SH Benson

The seven pints represented both the days of the week and the seven beneficial reasons for drinking *Guinness*: "strength, nerves, digestion, exhaustion, sleeplessness, its tonic effects and for the blood".

However, in this particular case, getting right under the skin of the product didn't provide the necessary inspiration. Greene and Bevan had also been conducting a series of informal polls in pubs. The leading question they put to drinkers was, "Why do you drink Guinness?", and the overwhelming response was simply, "Because it's good for you". This was the genesis of one of the most memorable advertising slogans of all time.

When Bensons presented its "Guinness is good for you" concept to the Guinness Board, they were initially met with scepticism. It was too simple, they complained. But that was the beauty of it. Mnemonic devices such as slogans or catchphrases are best kept to a few, easily digested words. If they are alliterative, rhyme or contain some form of in-built rhythm, so much the better. The classic sign-off lines which nag at you years after their demise tend to conform to these basic rules; consider, for instance, "You can be sure of Shell", "Drinka Pinta Milka Day", "Beanz Meanz Heinz" or "Unzip a banana". These slogans may be simple but their catchiness makes them difficult to forget.

The "Guinness is good for you" theme also neatly tapped into the nation's obsession with health. It's revealing to note quite how many products claimed restorative powers – some more convincingly than others – prior to the establishment of the National Health Service in 1948. In the 1920s and 1930s, small advertisements for "pick-me-ups", tonics and salts were commonplace, and posters for foods didn't tend to home in on taste or image as they do now, rather they stressed their positive effects on the constitution. A well-known 1920 poster for Bovril by the artist HH Harris (also through Bensons) shows a sleepy but totally unconcerned pyjama-clad man astride a sea-borne jar of Bovril; the accompanying slogan, almost inevitably, reads "prevents that sinking feeling".

The first "Guinness is good for you" poster campaign was tested in Scotland throughout 1928 and finally rolled out nationwide from Spring 1929, together with a series of press releases. Greene further refined the basic claim, compiling a list of seven beneficial reasons for drinking *Guinness*: it was apparently good for "strength, nerves, digestion, exhaustion, sleeplessness, its tonic effects and for the blood". The idea of *Guinness* miraculously boosting strength, like Popeye's spinach, was developed in the later "Guinness for Strength" campaign.

By the autumn of 1929, Bensons felt confident enough to release a new poster with just three monosyllabic words on it: "Good for You" – dispensing with the brand name altogether. In just a few months it had established an instantly recognisable advertising property: the graphic clues of the red upper-case sans-serif type, the black and green border and the lovingly painted glasses helped strengthen the message. There was another reason Bensons was able to get away with this almost advertising shorthand; as Tom Bury, Chief Executive Officer and Deputy Chairman of Guinness' previous advertising agency Ogilvy & Mather pointed out, "Guinness is a logo in a glass".

Press advertisement 1930

Agency SH Benson

After it had been established that *Guinness* was "Good for You", the next step was to show the beer as being refreshing and enjoyable to drink as well.

With the "Good for You" iconography and underlying intent having become firmly rooted in public consciousness, Bensons could easily afford to introduce variations on the medicinal theme such as "A Guinness a day", and "Have a Guinness when you're tired". So was there any justification behind Bensons' medicinal claims? Quite possibly. The alcohol content of *Guinness* is low enough for it to have a

There's nothing like a GUINNESS

Poster 1938

Agency SH Benson

The smiling head was a compromise between the early naturalistic illustrations of pint glasses and the later comic style that Gilroy adopted with his animal characters.

relaxing effect, while its iron content is high. In Ireland, *Guinness* is still given to blood donors and stomach and intestinal post-operative patients, a practice that was halted some time ago in Britain. For many years it was recommended to pregnant women and nursing mothers, though it is current medical policy to advise abstinence from alcohol if pregnant or breast-feeding. Whatever the truth of the matter, Bensons' early advertising strategy successfully perpetuated the existing folklore surrounding the → p. 023

Poster 1950

Agency SH Benson

Over the years, Bensons re-used their best
advertising images repeatedly, but with slight
variations. In this case the "Guinness Time" theme
and the smiling pint face have been combined.

Poster 1931

Agency SH Benson

The "Guinness Time" campaign was developed in 1931 after an illuminated electric *Guinness* branded clock was put up in Piccadilly Circus, London. *Guinness* branded clocks were erected in several other British cities and became popular meeting places.

Poster 1934

Agency SH Benson

By 1934 the basic graphic vocabulary for the posters had been established: a simple white background, a black and green border, a red sans-serif typeface and a witty image.

Press advertisement 1933

Agency SH Benson

Artist J Gilroy

Guinness and oysters is a long-standing Irish culinary tradition.
Bensons first used the idea of oysters in 1929, when they
adapted the story of the Walrus and the Carpenter from Lewis
Carroll's *Through the Looking Glass* for a press advertisement.

GUINNESS TIME

Have this one with me !

Poster 1935
Agency SH Benson
This slightly surreal poster promoted *Guinness* as an accompaniment to crab.

drink while extending brand awareness to a mass audience. The slogan "Guinness is good for you" was used extensively on posters until 1937, and sporadically in specialist press advertisements until the late 1960s. It also laid the foundations for some of the most celebrated poster advertising of all time. □

Doctors' books

Bensons actively sought testimonials from doctors in order to substantiate and give credibility to the "Guinness is good for you" proposition. Thousands were happy to oblige. The best of these encomiums were duly reproduced in press advertisements and bottle labels. "A bottle of Guinness put in front of, say a dispirited, health-greedy convalescent has a wonderfully auto-suggestive, cheer-producing effect," wrote one. "It contains nearly seven per cent of solid matter in solution and is therefore a food as well as a stimulant and tonic," concluded another.

As a means of encouraging the relationship and fostering goodwill, the agency hit upon the idea of producing collectable, limited-edition soft-back booklets which were sent out to doctors each Christmas from 1933 until 1939; the practice was revived after the war in 1950 and continued until 1966. The themed, lavishly illustrated books, notable for their whimsical charm and overt literary parody, contained many lateral – and often ingenious – references to *Guinness*, both visual and verbal.

The first Christmas book to reach doctors' surgeries was *The Guinness Alice*, an immaculate parody of Lewis Carroll's Alice books written by Ronald Barton and Robert Bevan, and illustrated by John Gilroy. Music hall, mad inventions, Gilbert and Sullivan and DIY provided the focus for other books in the series, though the redoubtable Alice was revisited on another four occasions.

The crime novelist Dorothy L Sayers, who was employed in Bensons' creative department from 1922 to 1929, contributed to some of the earlier Doctors' Books. The copywriter Stanley Penn took the lead during the 1950s and 1960s, writing ten books in successive years. The words were erudite enough, but the illustrations that accompanied them were impeccable.

The subtle humour and intricate scene-setting of artists Rex Whistler and Antony Groves-Raines (who illustrated eight of the *Guinness* Christmas books) set the early post-war pace. These were later superseded by a more directly comic approach epitomised by the somewhat eccentric work of cartoonists Rowland Emett and Gerard Hoffnung. Bernard Lodge, a pioneer in television graphics who was responsible for the award-winning *Dr Who* title sequence, is credited (along with Maureen Roffey) with the illustrations for the 1963 Christmas book, *Guinness Nonscience*, which introduced an arresting graphic approach.

The Guinness Legends 1934

Artist J Gilroy

Popular verses were skilfully parodied in the
second Doctors' Book, with plenty of references
to *Guinness*.

Guinness Nonscience 1963

Artists M Roffey and B Lodge

The cover illustration marks a radical departure in
the style of the Doctors' Books and depicts a robot
holding a glass of *Guinness*.

" Then its Use—you may serve it with oysters or cheese,
      At dinner, or lunch—or alone ;
And its Goodness, for treating yourself and your friends,
      And promoting digestion and tone.

" The fifth is the Colour, akin to Vandyke,
      Or rubies of opulent flame ;
And the sixth—the low Price, for a drink that's so nice ;
      And the seventh, and last, is the Name.

" For although other Stout does exist without doubt,
      Yet I feel it my duty to say,
When it's GUINNESS—"
                  —the Bellman broke off with a shout,
      For his hearers had hastened away.

He sought them with corkscrews,
                        he sought them with care,
      He pursued them with jugs and speed
To the "Garter and Star," where they'd opened the bar—
      A marvellous moment indeed !

In the midst of the words he was trying to say—
      'Mid sounds of rejoicing and glee,
They were merrily laughing and quaffing away—
      For the Stout *was* a GUINNESS you see !

***The Guinness Alice* 1933**

Artist J Gilroy

This illustration for the Hunting of the Stout
comes from the first Doctors' Book.

"You can't look at a taste, you know," said Alice, "but I suppose you mean that you like Guinness very much?"

"Of course we do," said Tweedledum. "Haven't we just said that there's nothing like it?"

***Jabberwocky Re-versed* 1935**

Artist J Gilroy

Gilroy perfectly imitated Tenniel's original drawings.

Daisy, Daisy

(To the tune of "Daisy, Daisy"))

Daisy, Daisy, give me a sandwich, do!
Don't be lazy, give me my Guinness, too!
For lunch isn't lunch without it,
So hurry up about it!
It's nice to drink
And it's nice to think
That a Guinness is good for you!

Songs of our
Grandfathers 1936
Artist R Whistler

Victorian popular
songs inspired this
Christmas book.

Prodigies and Prodigals 1939

Artist A Groves-Raines

A human pyramid supported by a strong man
illustrates the "Guinness for Strength" slogan.

Songs of our Grandfathers 1936

Artist R Whistler

Doctors' Books provided constant witty reminders
of the benefits of drinking *Guinness*.

That Britons always Rule the Waves,
And also Never shall be Slaves,
Are Laws. Another law we've heard
Demands a cautionary word.
It is: "that all things have their season."
Our book confirms this rule—in reason—
By showing clearly what one ought
To do, each month, by way of sport.
The verses also show—and you'll
Agree—that Guinness Waives the Rule.

A Guinness Sportfolio 1950
Artist A Groves-Raines

This sporting almanac was the first
Doctors' Book to be published after
World War II.

SPACE SHIP

Whatever worlds we visit
When we explore the sky,
There'll be nothing like a Guinness,
However far we fly.

So we'll have to take it with us
And thank our lucky stars
That we've got a stock of Goodness
For our rocket-tour to Mars.

And if we travel fast enough
Faster, say, than light,
We may catch up the Guinness
That we didn't have last night.

What Will They Think of Next? 1954
Artist A Groves-Raines

The artist created plasticine models of
scenes for his illustrations to achieve a
three-dimensional effect.

By hook or by crook I'll be last in this book

Happy New Lear 1957

Artist J Nash

The smiling face on the glass of *Guinness*
was a device to make it look more inviting.

Although they say
The Cathode Ray
Has stifled all endeavour.
That no pursuit
Will now take root—
Hobbies have gone for ever.

Less jaundiced, we
Do not agree—
With this prognostication,
And Guinness now
Set out to show
The joys of recreation,
As practised by a family,
That could belong to you or me.

Hobby Horses 1958

Artist R Emett

Rowland Emett illustrated this book of verses
about curious pastimes.

Alice Versary 1959

Artist R Ferns

The last Carrollian *Guinness* book appeared in the
company's bicentennial year.

My Goodness! My Gilbert and Sullivan! 1961

Artist A Groves-Raines

Copywriter Stanley Penn adapted Gilbert and
Sullivan's operettas to advertise *Guinness*.

Tail Piece

Be sure to get your little pet
It's favourite habitat,
A bosom for your viper,
A belfry for your bat.

Crickets like a cosy hearth,
A bonnet's best for bees.
A manger for your dog, of course.
An ear is marked for fleas.

And if you're keeping Guinness,
Select with care a spot
That's not too cold in winter,
In summer, not too hot.

***Reigning Cats & Dogs* 1960**

Artist G Hoffnung

Due to his early death, this was Hoffnung's
only book for Guinness.

My goodness, my Guinness

Posters are one of the oldest and arguably the purest form of advertising. The essence of their message must be conveyed with clarity, immediacy and impact. They are literally speaking to the "man in the street", and the best examples of the genre manage to achieve a contemporary, populist appeal. The art historian John Barnicoat writes that, "The [poster] designer ... must achieve instant contact. To do this he must, like the entertainer, work with his audience. In many cases it becomes necessary to speak to the unprofessional audience in a popular way, although there are times when an audience expects a degree of technical brilliance."

Poster 1939

Agency SH Benson

Artist J Gilroy

The seven bottles in the pelican's beak
allude to the "Guinness a day" slogan.

On Guinness' behalf, the artist John Gilroy, with an elegance and fluidity which belies the complexities involved, managed to combine accessibility with wit and consummate draughtsmanship. Gilroy's work on SH Bensons' "Guinness for Strength" and "My goodness, my Guinness" campaigns of the 1930s and 1940s remain some of the most potent and evocative advertising images of all time.

The period between the wars was unquestionably the "Golden Age" of the advertising poster, and Gilroy's contribution to the burgeoning genre was significant. He was in good company. In Britain, the Surrealists Man Ray and Hans Schleger ("Zero") and the prolific American émigré E McKnight Kauffer were studiously redefining the discipline. In France, the Art Deco style of AM Cassandre and Jean Carlu was in vogue, while in the Soviet Union, the Constructivist artist and photographer Alexander Rodchenko was perfecting a radical synthesis of image and typography.

Few poster campaigns, however, have managed to encapsulate the mood and sensibilities of the British public as eloquently as Gilroy's long-running series for Guinness. "Guinness for strength" was a thematic development of the "Guinness is good for you" campaign, intended to give the drink a more masculine image. Strength was one of seven efficacious characteristics of Guinness that Bensons' Oswald Greene had earlier identified – the one which most obviously appealed to men. The campaign was also a gentle send-up of the premise underlying most advertising – that buying a product can transform the user into a better person: more attractive, sexually desirable, socially popular and powerful.

The inherent humour was, of course, achieved by simple exaggeration; after supping a Guinness you could apparently lift huge metal girders, pull a horse along in a cart or chop down a tree with the single blow of an axe. Gilroy's comic characters, the muscular blond woodsman and the nonchalant, flat-capped girder-carrier, are perfectly judged; they are barrel-chested and masculine, but ever-so-slightly mock-heroic. The astonished onlookers, amazed by these feats of strength, are more obvious foils and unmistakably comic in intent.

The "girder" poster was a triumph, spawning a host of parodies in the popular press at the time and endowing a pint of Guinness with a new nickname – "a girder". Gilroy managed to utilise the full width of the landscape format, while the angle of perspective makes the substantial metal girder look as if it is about to burst out from the confines of the illustration.

More significantly, Gilroy refined the graphic vocabulary of the Guinness poster, introducing a bold, colourful cartoon style – invariably on a simple white background – to complement the by-now distinctive type and bordering. This was to evolve into the celebrated "My goodness, my Guinness" campaign.

The antics of the harassed zoo-keeper and his mischievous charges are said to have been inspired by a visit Gilroy made to Bertram Mills's Circus in Olympia, though his sketches and studies of the various animals were made at London Zoo. The red-faced, moustachioed zoo-keeper was a caricature of the artist himself, as Gilroy seemingly displayed a Hitchcockian desire to appear as a cameo in his own work.

Poster 1937

Agency SH Benson
Artist J Gilroy

Once the format of the "My goodness, my Guinness" campaign had been established, Gilroy was able to create playful topical or seasonal variations.

Poster (proof) c 1930s

Agency SH Benson

Artist J Gilroy

This original artwork for a poster was not used. The slogan "I feel I need a Guinness" and the straight-forward representation of a worker reaching for a pint of *Guinness* lacked the wit of other works by Gilroy.

Poster (proof) 1932

Agency SH Benson

Artist J Gilroy

Gilroy made portrait and landscape versions of many of his most famous posters. This particularly long version of the statue cleaner poster shows how well he managed to combine a sense of the painterly with effective graphic design.

The first poster in the highly durable campaign was launched in 1935, and featured a sea lion making off with a pint of *Guinness* perched on its nose. It provided the basis for innumerable variants which saw the hapless keeper pitting his wits against kangaroos, ostriches, giraffes, pelicans, gnus and lions, all of whom were determined to hijack his precious *Guinness*.

The new slogan worked on several different levels: the word "goodness" playing on the word "Guinness" and harking back to the original "Guinness is good for you" line. As an exclamation, "Goodness!" highlighted the drama of the accompanying visual scenario. It was both alliterative and rhythmically symmetrical. There was a slight tweak in the typographical styling too; the red letters were

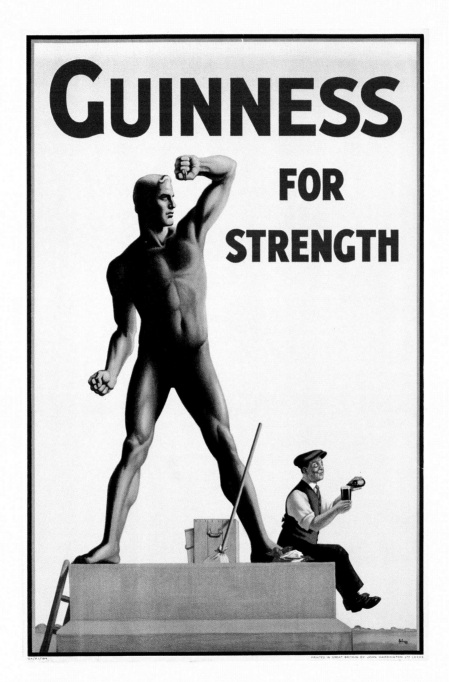

Poster 1932

Agency SH Benson

Artist J Gilroy

The portrait version of the statue cleaner poster is the most familiar. Gilroy completed several detailed anatomical sketches before he was finally satisfied with the proportions of the statue of Hercules.

Poster 1934

Agency SH Benson

Artist J Gilroy

The workman carrying the girder became one of
the most celebrated advertising posters of all time.
It was revamped and adapted by advertising agency
J Walter Thompson in 1976 with a new strapline:
"Guinness. It's as long as you can remember".

italicised, subtly emphasising the movement and
action in the comic tableaux.

In the 26 years of the campaign, there was a
discernible development in Gilroy's illustrative
technique. Early posters were more stylised, with flat
colours and two-dimensional comic-book style
rendering; there was a definite nod to Art Deco, the

fashionable idiom of the era. Later executions tended
to be more rounded and painterly, the creatures' eyes
the only concession to artistic licence, though even
they had become markedly smaller over the years.

The introduction of the animals proved to be a
masterstroke. The toucan, for example, created by
Gilroy in 1935 and part of the *Guinness* menagerie for

ILLUSTRATED SPORTING & DRAMATIC ... April 7.
TATLER ... ... November 14.

"I'd give
the world for
a Guinness"

GUINNESS
for STRENGTH

G.E. 369A

Press advertisement (proof) 1934
Agency SH Benson
Artist J Gilroy

A secondary copy line, "I'd give the
world for a Guinness", was introduced
for a magazine advertisement. Its context
allowed Gilroy to introduce more detail
than his posters, which required a greater
level of immediacy and impact.

over 25 years, rose again in 1979 to front a take-home sales campaign and became popular in the company's television advertisements in the early 1980s. The animals appealed to a broad range of socio-cultural groups, and catapulted *Guinness* advertising into mainstream popular culture. The campaign was also easily adapted to topical and seasonal variations. The public eagerly awaited Gilroy's every move and reacted enthusiastically to what they thought were erroneous details. Many pointed out, for example, that the glass in the famous ostrich poster was the wrong way up in the bird's neck (see page 45). The artist was a stickler, however, undertaking numerous versions before he was satisfied, so they very rarely caught him out. Even if they did, Gilroy usually had a plausible explanation.

Sketch c 1935
Agency SH Benson
Artist J Gilroy

Gilroy's rough
sketches were for a
rejected poster idea.

Poster 1935

Agency SH Benson
Artist J Gilroy

The first – and arguably finest – poster
in the Gilroy zoo-keeper and animal
series. The first *Guinness* television
commercial, broadcast in 1955 on ITV's
inaugural night, enacted the same scene
with the actor Charles Naughton playing
the zoo-keeper and a live sea lion.

Like the "Guinness for Strength" campaign before it,
"My goodness, my Guinness" was seized upon with
alacrity and adapted by contemporary political
cartoonists, which only reinforced the message
of the originals.

The slogan quickly became a catchphrase of the day,
generating unprecedented levels of publicity for the
product. It is every advertising agency's dream to
create a campaign that passes into the vernacular, but
few actually achieve it. □

Poster 1936

Agency SH Benson
Artist J Gilroy

The tortoise was
an appropriate
candidate to
promote *Guinness*
as a pick-me-up.

Poster 1936

Agency SH Benson
Artist J Gilroy

Gilroy deliberately drew the glass upright in the ostrich's neck
to make sure that the outline looked like a glass. However,
members of the public still insisted on writing letters
complaining that if the ostrich had drunk the pint, the glass
would be the other way up. Gilroy explained that the ostrich
had been copying the sea lion, unsuccesfully attempting to
balance the pint on its nose before swallowing it whole.

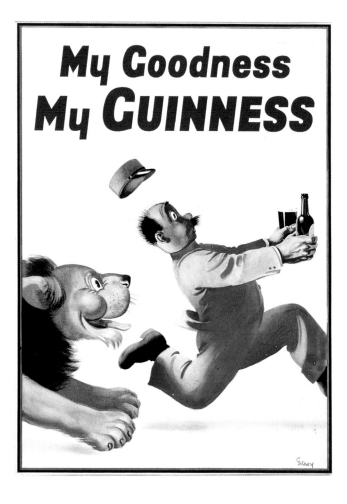

Poster 1937
Agency SH Benson
Artist J Gilroy

The lion used in this poster was one of the least popular of Gilroy's animals.

Sketch c 1930s
Agency SH Benson
Artist J Gilroy

This colour sketch of an animal scene was never used as a poster. Gilroy sketched dozens of different animals for the "My goodness, my Guinness" campaign, many of which progressed no further than the drawing board.

Poster 1938

Agency SH Benson
Artist J Gilroy

This poster was a
variation on the
zoo-keeper theme.

If he can say as you can
Guinness is good for you
How grand to be a Toucan
Just think what Toucan do

G E 490 L

Poster 1935

Agency SH Benson
Artist J Gilroy

This advertisement presented
the *Guinness* toucan for the
first time, with words courtesy
of Dorothy L Sayers.

Sketch c 1937

Agency SH Benson

Artist J Gilroy

This was an earlier sketch of
what was to become the
"woodcutter" poster shown
alongside.

Poster 1937

Agency SH Benson

Artist J Gilroy

Some members of the public thought that the
lumberjack's axe was being held the wrong way
round, so Bensons went to the trouble of
sending diagrams to correspondents
demonstrating the accuracy of the picture.

Poster 1951

Agency SH Benson

Artist "Wilk"(Dick Wilkinson)

After Gilroy left Bensons to go freelance in the 1940s, the agency started to use other artists. However, Gilroy's influence in both the subject matter and style can be seen in this poster by "Wilk". The copywriter John Trench devised the idea for the poster and the "123 HUP" registration number plate.

Poster 1949

Agency SH Benson

Artist J Gilroy

When this poster first appeared it was so successful that Gilroy
was given a standing ovation when he walked into the Garrick
Club in London. The poster was Gilroy's personal favourite.

Poster 1952

Agency SH Benson
Artist J Gilroy

Several bill-posters pasted
the kinkajou poster
upside-down.

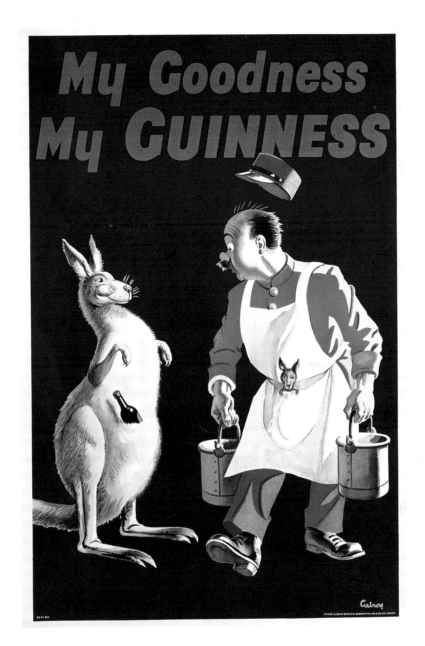

Poster 1943

Agency SH Benson

Artist J Gilroy

A black-and-white line-drawn version
of this scene was first used as a press
advertisement in 1942. The poster version was
re-issued in 1947 but with a light background.

Poster 1954

Agency SH Benson

Artist J Gilroy

This poster's familiarity relied on John
Gilroy's original sealion and zoo keeper
poster of 1935 (page 43).

My Goodness – My GUINNESS

Poster 1956

Agency SH Benson
Artist J Gilroy

Gilroy played down the ferocity of certain animals by giving them a cartoon flavour. Here, the bear's eyes and lower lip are comically exaggerated.

Artwork 1953

Agency SH Benson

Artist J Gilroy

To celebrate the Coronation of Queen
Elizabeth II on 2 June 1953, John Gilroy
and Bensons' copywriter Stanley Penn
devised this poster. It brought together all
the favourite *Guinness* animals and became
the first British poster to have neither copy
nor any reference to the product.

Sketch 1950s

Artist J Gilroy

This sketch was made for a
trophy for a Guinness-
sponsored bowls
competition. An
enduring *Guinness*
icon, the irrepressible
bird gradually became
more cartoonesque.

Guinness Time

Poster 1958

Agency SH Benson
Artist J Gilroy

The last few posters Gilroy painted for Guinness tended to feature all his animals together. By the late 1950s Bensons was increasingly turning to other illustrators for its poster art.

Alice in Wonderland

Between 1929 and 1959, a secondary campaign, inspired by Lewis Carroll's *Alice's Adventures in Wonderland* and *Through the Looking Glass* books, ran in tandem with Guinness' mainstream advertising. Its tone and style was at odds with the slapstick of John Gilroy's "My goodness, my Guinness" work and the macho leanings of the "Guinness for Strength" posters.

In the context of today's emphasis on coherent, through-the-line advertising strategy, the "Alice" campaign would no doubt be perceived as gratuitous, an unnecessary distraction from the brand's core values, but at the time, it served to heighten the charm and sense of mystique surrounding *Guinness.*

Moreover, it gave Bensons' ranks of erudite copywriters, many of whom would have been just as much at home in an Oxbridge Senior Common Room, the opportunity to indulge in one of their favourite pastimes – literary parody. They constantly strove to outshine each other, crafting a crisp catalogue of verses which alluded to previous *Guinness* advertisements as well as the extremely curious goings-on in the Alice fables. " 'Off with his head!' cried the queen. 'Nonsense,' cried Alice. 'Guinness always keeps its head.' ", in a neat reworking from 1932, which concludes with the executioner exiting with a *Guinness* "head and all".

The illustrations for the "Alice" campaign were outstanding. Gilroy mimicked the style of John Tenniel's original drawings, before adding his own slant; Antony Groves-Raines, for his part, introduced a meticulous cod-Victorian look, which reached its height in the Christmas book, *Alice Aforethought – Guinness Carrolls for 1938.*

But *Guinness* and Alice didn't enjoy an entirely blissful marriage. Early on in the affair, Macmillan & Co., the publishers of the Alice books, raised the thorny subject of copyright with Bensons – however, after much conjecture, they eventually concluded that they could enjoy a mutually beneficial relationship with the advertisers.

The last official "Alice" *Guinness* advertisement appeared in 1959, but she was dusted off again in 1965, to celebrate the hundredth anniversary of the publication of *Alice's Adventures in Wonderland.* "Among the many who owe a debt to Lewis Carroll was Guinness," ran the copy. "In the 1930s a series of Alice parodies appeared which were so well received that two of them are preserved in the British Museum Library. Guinness and Alice have since gone their separate ways; we at Guinness look back at those days with affection, and we remember this anniversary with gratitude and respect." A fitting codicil, with Bensons giving themselves a well deserved pat on the back.

District Railway panel posters 1930s–1940s

Agency SH Benson

Artist J Gilroy

The Alice parodies were originally instituted as a means of advertising *Guinness* and oysters, but their remit and subject matter quickly widened.

World War II

Even advertising was rationed during World War II. Restrictions were imposed on the sizes of poster and press advertisements, and special permission was required for the publication of advertising leaflets and catalogues. The Ministry of Information (MOI), under the supervision of Lord Macmillan, was easily the biggest advertiser during this period, reminding the public in no uncertain terms that "Careless talk costs lives", and that every honest subject had a responsibility to the war effort. Between March 1940 and June 1945, the government was estimated to have spent £9.5 million on public service advertising.

SH Benson, which relocated from central London to the relative safety of Rickmansworth for the duration of the war, was one of six agencies involved in the extensive "Squander bug" campaign. This featured a noxious, wasteful, insect-like character and exhorted the public to spend less and conserve resources – there was a wonderful irony in advertising agencies making a stand against consumption.

In *Keep Mum! Advertising Goes to War*, George Begley writes, "Suppliers of consumer goods, with the feeling of being on something to nothing, poured out hundreds of advertisements, of which the gist was: 'Let us remind you that we still exist, but for heaven's sake don't try to buy our goods.'" *Guinness* advertising was also sensitive to the war-time deprivations, but took a slightly different tack, using the humour of the familiar "My goodness, my Guinness" and "Guinness for Strength" campaigns to lift public morale and to support the cause.

There was an acute shortage of paper in Britain at the time, a problem that Bensons ingeniously circumvented by printing new posters on the back of old ones. On occasion, this meant that the usual *Guinness* colour scheme had to be compromised, incorporating dark backgrounds to cover up the show through from the other side. But this was a small price to pay for a continuous advertising presence in extremely trying circumstances.

Guinness' war-time advertising was made possible only by the momentum of its earlier work. Existing slogans and characters proved highly adaptable, and there was a certain comfort in their familiarity.

Gilroy's zoo-keeper was transformed into a Home Guard volunteer, but still managed to get into his usual scrapes; his customary look of panic in evidence as his full bottle of precious *Guinness* is mistakenly lobbed into the air during a Molotov cocktail throwing exercise. "Guinness for Strength" was adapted to boost the productivity drive.

Artwork 1941

Agency SH Benson
Artist J Gilroy

A dive-bombing Spitfire provided
a wartime variation on the "My
goodness, my Guinness" slogan.

Playing on the MOI's famous "Dig for
Victory" campaign, a farmer is shown
merrily pushing a large wheelbarrow which
was packed ridiculously high with produce.

The cartoonist HM Bateman created a
succession of light-hearted army-based
scenarios: a general pulling rank over a
sergeant for his pint; a platoon on the march
takes a fork in the road towards a tempting
Guinness poster inscribed with, "Thousands
are turning to Guinness for strength".

However, it was a 1941 window display
featuring the "smiling head" of *Guinness*
which really set the tone. The tight-lipped
smile and arched eyebrows are distinctly
stoical, but the copy line underneath reads,
"Guinness as usual".

The same was true of Bensons' advertising during this period. In a typically
humorous, understated manner, it did its
utmost to make the best of what was a
difficult period.

Artwork 1942

Agency SH Benson
Artist J Gilroy

In the above artwork, Gilroy's zoo-keeper in his Home Guard role supervised a Molotov cocktail throwing session.

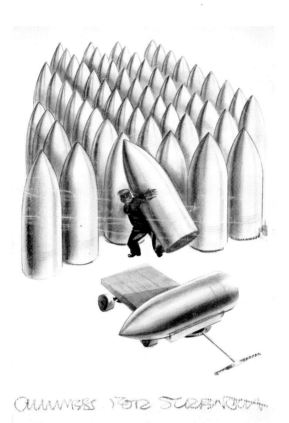

Sketch c 1940

Agency SH Benson
Artist J Gilroy

A sailor loading shells single-handedly promoted "Guinness for Strength".

Sketch c 1940

Agency SH Benson
Artist J Gilroy

Gilroy toyed with the idea of depicting the nation's leaders – in this sketch a Churchillian bulldog made off with Hitler's *Guinness*. This particular idea was never actually published.

"My Goodness — My Guinness"

Press advertisement c 1942

Agency SH Benson

Artist HM Bateman

HM Bateman's war-time cartoons used
the established slogans, but took *Guinness*
into the world of the army barracks.

Press advertisement 1942

Agency SH Benson

Artist HM Bateman

Guinness advertising became self-
referential in another of Bateman's
humorous takes on army life.

"*I would now like someone to help me make this Guinness disappear.*"

My Goodness — My GUINNESS

G.E.1181.A

Press advertisement 1944

Agency SH Benson

Artist HM Bateman

Light-hearted advertisements that indicated the popularity of *Guinness* helped to raise morale.

My Goodness—My GUINNESS

Press advertisement 1943

Agency SH Benson
Artist J Gilroy

Gilroy gave a naval slant to the "My goodness, my Guinness" idea.

"I feel like a GUINNESS!"
"I wish you were!"

Press advertisement 1944

Agency SH Benson
Artist J Gilroy

Old *Guinness* jokes were reworked for the war effort.

DIG FOR ~~VICTORY~~ *PLENTY*

GUINNESS for STRENGTH

Poster 1945

Agency SH Benson

Artist J Gilroy

The Ministry of Information's "Dig for Victory" slogan was adapted and integrated into the "Guinness for Strength" campaign.

John Gilroy, MA, ARCA, FRSA

In 1925, 27-year-old John Gilroy joined SH Bensons' creative department as an "in-house artist", a position that has completely disappeared from the television-centric agencies of the 1990s. After completing minor projects for Skipper Sardines and Virol, he was put to work on the high-profile Colman's "Mustard Club" campaign of 1926, collaborating with fellow artist William Brearley and the copywriters Oswald Greene and Dorothy L Sayers. It was a tentative example of the amusing, character-based advertising at which he excelled, with press and posters introducing an enthusiastic public to the entertaining Baron de Beef and Miss Di Gester.

Gilroy went on to tackle campaigns for Bovril, Macleans toothpaste and Monk & Glass Custard, but without question, it was his work on behalf of *Guinness* stout for which he is best remembered. Over a period of 35 years, he created well over 100 press and poster advertisements for *Guinness*. Among them are two of the most enduring advertising images ever crafted: a workman casually carrying a huge girder on his shoulder for the "Guinness for Strength" campaign, and the impudent sea lion making off with the zoo-keeper's pint in the inaugural "My goodness, my Guinness" poster. Interviewed in the latter stages of his career, Gilroy remarked, with typical modesty, "I have always been a jolly man and I thought the Guinness campaign needed a touch of humour."

Gilroy was born in 1898 at Whitley Bay, Newcastle-upon-Tyne, one of eight children. His father, also called John, was a marine landscape painter and technical draftsman, who young Gilroy quickly decided to emulate. He honed his drawing skills by copying cartoons from *Punch*, and by the age of 15 was contributing caricatures of local celebrities to the *Newcastle Evening Chronicle*. Gilroy duly won a scholarship to Armstrong College Art School, Durham University, but his studies were interrupted by the outbreak of World War I. He joined the Royal Field Artillery, and served in France, Italy and Palestine. After the war, Gilroy accepted a place at the Royal College of Art, winning several more scholarships

John Gilroy 1934

The artist produced over 100 posters and press advertisements for *Guinness* over a period of 35 years.

Sketch c 1930s
Artist J Gilroy

A rough sketch for a potential *Guinness* poster.

Bensons' Studio 1935

Advertisements for Bovril and Gold Flake tobacco, as well as the first "My goodness, my Guinness" poster featuring the sea lion and the zoo-keeper, line the walls of Bensons' London studio.

during his tenure, and staying on to teach until he joined Bensons in 1925. He left the agency in the 1940s, but continued producing *Guinness* advertisements on a freelance basis well into the 1960s.

His versatility and technical skills were remarkable. He had the ability to flit with consummate ease from intricate pen-and-ink line drawings – as featured in the *Guinness* Doctors' Christmas Books – to the expansive canvas of the poster, and was as happy painting murals as greetings cards. But Gilroy also had a reputation as an accomplished landscape and portrait

Sketch c 1930s

Artist J Gilroy

Gilroy's concept for a snooker-based advertisement was later developed by J Walter Thompson in the 1970s.

Sketch c 1930s

Artist J Gilroy

This sketch presented a further exploration of the "strength" theme.

Sketch c 1930s

Artist J Gilroy

The idea for this sketch certainly wouldn't get past today's regulatory bodies.

Sketch c 1950s

Artist J Gilroy

This rejected poster idea parodied the distinctive sculpture of Henry Moore.

Artwork c 1932

Artist J Gilroy

This artwork for a "strength" poster featured two Covent Garden porters. The accompanying verse concluded: *Guinness...* "brings the house down every time".

Sketch c 1936

Artist J Gilroy

The rhinoceros
never became a
fully fledged
member of the
Guinness zoo.

Artwork 1959

Artist J Gilroy

This artwork was for a
press advertisement
for Draught *Guinness*.

Sketch c 1930s
Artist J Gilroy

These preliminary sketches were for an idea which was later abandoned.

Sketch c 1930s
Artist J Gilroy

Along with a beaver, a bull, a woodpecker and a pack of racing grey-hounds, the camel never made it on to the advertising hoardings.

painter; his work was regularly exhibited at the Royal Academy, and his sitters included several members of the Royal Family, Sir Winston Churchill and Rupert Guinness, Lord Iveagh II.

Gilroy will probably be best remembered for his *Guinness* posters, which he constructed on the following no-nonsense premise: "Posters are a kind of aesthetic meal-in-a-minute. The man in the street is usually in a hurry to catch a bus or avoid being caught by one, and has no time for lengthy contemplation."*

Even today the humour and immediacy that Gilroy managed to achieve in his posters seem as fresh as ever.

* *Guinness Time, vol. 5, no. 2 Spring 1952, p19*

Lovely day for a Guinness

The graphic aesthetic

Advertising research and measurement techniques became widespread during the mid- to late 1950s, as British agencies took their cue from their progressive counterparts in the USA. The industry took on a more critical, quasi-scientific aspect, as the gentle eccentricity epitomised by John Gilroy and his contemporaries at Bensons was gradually squeezed out. Television was soon to pose a serious challenge to the traditional advertising media of press and posters. The NBC network began broadcasting in the US in 1946, and within three years had spawned 50 competitors. Commercial television had arrived in the UK by September 1955.

DOWN WITH GUINNESS!

– then you'll feel better

GA/PI/2110   PRINTED IN GT. BRITAIN BY SILK SCREEN ARTS LTD. CROYDON

Poster 1955

Agency SH Benson

The Bensons' copywriter
Stanley Penn conceived this
poster for the 1955 General
Election. It was printed and
held in store until the
date of the election was
announced, and then rolled
out across the country.
Typographic styling, colour
branding and pithy copy-
writing had become as
important as striking
imagery in poster design.

American commentator Vance Packard's seminal treatise, *The Hidden Persuaders* (1957), showed advertising's remit moving away from simple visual aesthetics and towards psychology. "Sex" and "the subliminal" were the new advertising buzzwords. It even hinted at sinister, covert practices in the industry, alleging that, "large-scale efforts are being made, often with impressive success, to channel our thinking habits, our purchasing decisions and our thought processes." A fanciful conspiracy theory? By no means.

Psychology had certainly become advertising's newest and most formidable ally. Guinness, in common with many go-ahead companies of this period, enlisted the help of a psychiatrist to get to grips with the mind-set of its target market. Dr FE Emery of the Tavistock Institute of Human Behaviour examined the evidence and duly compartmentalised beer drinkers into three main groups: "indulgent", "social" and "reparative" – the latter being a term coined by the eminent Freudian Melanie Klein. Most *Guinness* drinkers, Emery concluded, were "reparative": that is, they enjoyed a quiet drink in the evening as a reward for a hard day's work; they tended to be steady, responsible drinkers, the kind of people who knew their own minds and were happy with their lot.

This theory appeared to support the findings of earlier Guinness-commissioned surveys by Gallup and Mass Observation, as well as studies conducted by in-house market researcher George Wigglesworth, who had examined the demographics and consumption patterns of *Guinness* drinkers.

At Bensons, meanwhile, the guard was changing. A painful transformation took place as a new breed of go-getting advertising man emerged, conversant with the latest techniques and keen to exploit their knowledge. Gilroy's characters, which had served Guinness so well and for so long, were now deemed too quaint and old-fashioned to spearhead the next phase of *Guinness* advertising, and a new thrusting graphic vocabulary was sought to address the recently defined "reparative" drinker.

Though Gilroy continued to produce *Guinness* posters into the early 1960s, a variety of freelance designers were also invited to contribute. Two of them are particularly worthy of note. Tom Eckersley and Abram Games had both come to prominence during the war years, working for the Ministry of Information, and though their styles differed, they shared an ability to distil complex ideas into direct graphic statements.

Eckersley was awarded an OBE in 1949 for his services to British poster design, having produced influential work for Shell, London Transport and the General Post Office. Later, he became head of the graphic design department of the London College of Printing, where he remained for nearly 20 years (1957–1976). His work is characterised by a witty typographic playfulness and bold, highly stylised illustration. Bright, simple shapes are carefully positioned to achieve a form of ingenious visual shorthand.

His 1961 "After Work" poster (page 87) is a classic example. It comprises five basic components: a face, two shoe soles, a hand and a pint of *Guinness*. The drawing is rudimentary, child-like even, but the elements combine to put over an unmistakable message, that a pint of *Guinness* after work is both relaxing and rewarding. The scale and positioning of the soles are inspired; *Guinness* is instantly associated with putting your feet up. In "Lovely day for a

A. GAMES.

uinness

Poster 1957

Agency SH Benson
Artist A Games

Abram Games sketched
this ingenious design on
the back of a bus ticket.
After its release, it won
design awards in Helsinki,
Lisbon, New York,
Stockholm and Barcelona.

My Goodness!

SEE THE
GUINNESS FESTIVAL CLOCK

Poster 1951

Agency SH Benson

This poster was designed to encourage people to visit the *Guinness* Festival Clock, created for the Festival of Britain Pleasure Gardens in Battersea Park, London, in the summer of 1951. Every fifteen minutes the clock would burst into life: the sun spun round, the keeper rose from under an umbrella, the ostrich emerged from a chimney, marionettes revolved around a whirligig, the Mad Hatter came out of his house, and, finally, two toucans came out to peck at a *Guinness* Time Tree.

Guinness", an Eckersley poster from 1956, an absent-minded gardener is seen clipping a hedge in the shape of a sea lion with a pint of *Guinness* on its nose. It is an elegant transition, acknowledging the Gilroy heritage, but subtly introducing the new "reparative" motif. Our hobbyist may well have just returned home from work, and what he is thinking about is quite apparent.

During World War II, Abram Games had been appointed Official War Poster Designer and had established himself as one of the country's foremost practitioners. His work was the manifestation of his personal graphic philosophy, namely, "maximum meaning by minimum means". Games believed that, "The message must be given quickly and vividly so that interest is subconsciously retained...

Opening Time is
GUINNESS
TIME

Poster 1956

Agency SH Benson
Artist Lander

Though it wasn't by John Gilroy, this poster patently draws on the influence of his posters. The solid sans-serif typefaces, the use of green and red and the naturalistic style of painting are all hallmarks of Gilroy's work for Guinness.

The designer constructs, winds the spring. The viewer's eye is caught, the spring is released." Games's most effective poster for Guinness was his most simple: a huge red sans-serif "G" which has been doodled over to form a smiling face with a pint of *Guinness*. The pint glass fits neatly into the spur of the letter, the smile follows the curve of the base, a single stroke cuts across its crown, suggesting a bowler hat. This piece of typographic virtuosity was justifiably showered with international awards.

The positive reception accorded to Guinness' new graphic approach proved that there was life after Gilroy. His very last animal poster appeared in 1961, as the vogue for photographic representation in poster advertising began to take hold. □

Lovely day for a GUINNESS

Poster 1956

Agency SH Benson
Artist T Eckersley

There was a nod to
Gilroy in the topiary,
but Eckersley had a
far more direct
graphic approach,
incorporating flat
colours and a stylised
visual shorthand.

ECKERSLEY

Poster 1958

Agency SH Benson
Artist "Victoria"
(Victoria Davidson)

In this poster, brand iconography (the *Guinness* harp and bottle) was seamlessly incorporated into a fanciful scenario.

MILLION
GUINNESS
for strength every day

Poster 1960

Agency SH Benson

Artist J Gilroy

With the advent of television advertising, Guinness initiated a commercials campaign using the endline, "No wonder five million Guinnesses are enjoyed every day." In one of Gilroy's final works for Guinness, he adapted what was probably his most famous poster – the man with the girder – to illustrate the newly introduced copyline.

A. GAMES.

Poster 1960

Agency SH Benson
Artist A Games

Abram Games's approach to the "five million daily" campaign was entirely graphic. His play on the letter "G" and the inverted text anticipated later *Guinness* advertisements of 1965, which showed a series of evocative words such as "strong", "deep" and "good" printed both horizontally and vertically.

Press advertisement 1960

Agency SH Benson

This blatant pastiche, "It's so invigorating", echoed John
Hassall's classic "It's so bracing" Skegness poster of 1908.

GUINNESS

- the ideal summer resort

Poster 1961

Agency SH Benson
Artist J Gilroy

In John Gilroy's final *Guinness* poster, the animals appeared increasingly dated as a more rigorous approach to advertising began to take hold.

Poster 1961
Agency SH Benson

In 1961, Bensons began to target specific sections of the beer market. Poster imagery changed dramatically. The animals were dropped in favour of images of *Guinness* drinkers. One of the first of the new-look posters shows a "working-class" drinker on the shoulders of a "middle-class" drinker in a bid to appeal to members of both classes.

Poster 1961

Agency SH Benson
Artist T Eckersley

By using just four simple
graphic elements, this poster
conveys its message clearly –
after work, there is nothing
more relaxing or rewarding
than putting your feet up and
having a pint of Guinness.

Poster 1962

Agency SH Benson
Design B Hobbs

Bruce Hobbs
designed a series of
posters depicting
different types of
Guinness drinkers.

GOODNESS! GUINNESS!

Poster 1962
Agency SH Benson
Artist R Peppé

Peppé, working in an illustrative style close to Tom Eckersley's, contrived a variation on the familiar "My goodness, my Guinness" theme, and portrayed another *Guinness* drinker.

Cartoons

Cartoons, rather like printed advertisements, require a dynamic synergy of words and image. They share certain conventions too. A cartoon's punchline can be likened to an endline or slogan, for instance, and they both employ humour to disseminate a more serious underlying message. In the case of cartoons, this message may be socio-political or satirical; print advertisements, on the other hand, are simply pictorial vehicles of persuasion, whose object is to sell more product or reinforce brand values.

Guinness advertising has always fully exploited this crossover by commissioning a series of leading cartoonists to contribute to press campaigns and below-the-line material, including books, calendars and point-of-purchase items. Bensons began the tradition, utilising, among others, the varied talents of HM Bateman, Fougasse, Gerard Hoffnung, Rowland Emett and the ubiquitous John Gilroy.

In the 1970s, J Walter Thompson introduced cartoons by Mel Calman, Thelwell and Carl Giles, who were all prolific, high-profile exponents of the art. Even in the early 1990s, Ogilvy & Mather's "Fractionals" press and adshel (bus shelter) campaign, which were initiated by the agency art director Brian Fraser and featured droll doodles and captions, took its cue from the same tradition.

The diversity of approach and mannerisms of these illustrators is marked, but essentially they were performing a similar function on behalf of Guinness – complementing and developing the humorous intent of the lead campaign, while fostering a sense of goodwill toward the brand. The three cartoonists highlighted below illustrate the broad range of styles used to achieve the same ends.

The Australian-born HM Bateman (1887–1970) is probably best known for his contributions to *Punch* magazine. His forte was creating fairly complex one-off scenarios peopled by ruddy-faced protagonists. A cricket scene in which a puny, panic-stricken batsman squares up to a fiery muscle-bound bowler typifies Bateman's carefully constructed wit and rigorous attention to detail.

"Fougasse" (1887–1965) was the pseudonym of Cyril Kenneth Bird, who took his name from the French word for a small anti-personnel mine used during World War I, believing that cartoons relied on a similar minor explosive effect. Stylistically, his work was far less polished than Bateman's, but a few choice lines could suggest a fully comprehensible vignette. In a 1933 press advertisement picturing a pair of hikers hankering after a *Guinness*, Fougasse manages to conjure an undulating landscape with remarkable economy.

"I feel like a Guinness"
"I wish you were!"

Press advertisement 1933
Agency SH Benson
Artist "Fougasse" (CK Bird)

The "I feel like a Guinness" quip was
endlessly recycled in different situations.
Few, however, managed to conjure up a
scene with such economy and fluidity as
Fougasse's inspired line drawing.

Press advertisement 1936
Agency SH Benson
Artist J Gilroy

This is yet another example of Gilroy's
supreme draughtsmanship and versatility.

Bulbous, faux-naïf characters with
disproportionately large heads proved to be
cartoonist Mel Calman's stock-in-trade. A
selection of these characters was roped in to
lend some of their cosy charm to J Walter
Thompson's early 1970s "Give him a
Guinness" campaign. Even in the context of
Guinness advertising, Calman's conspicuous
style relies on incisive quips rather than the
quality of his draughtsmanship.

My Goodness—My GUINNESS

Artwork 1944

Artist HM Bateman

This rare two-part advertisement
by Bateman had a moral: never
take your eye off your *Guinness.*

Press advertisement 1944

Agency SH Benson
Artist J Hart

Cartoons proved a friendly and highly
flexible medium, allowing the messages
and flavour of the poster campaign to be
extended into press advertising.

The dream of the golfer who forgot
his GUINNESS a day
GUINNESS IS GOOD FOR YOU

Press advertisement 1946

Agency SH Benson

Artist HM Bateman

Bateman's popular golf and cricket cartoons originally
appeared in the 1937 doctors' book and were reused as
series of *Guinness* press advertisements in 1946.

Umpire: "Will you take middle or leg, Sir?"
Batsman: "I think I had better take a GUINNESS!"

Press advertisement 1946

Agency SH Benson

Artist HM Bateman

An oblique reference to the "Guinness for
Strength" campaign is conveyed by
typically red-cheeked Bateman characters.

Press advertisement 1966

Agency SH Benson

Role reversal was employed to inject humour into the original *Guinness* slogan. Cartoonists were given the "punchline" and worked backwards to create the structure of the joke.

Press advertisement 1961

Agency SH Benson

Here, a mixture of messages were combined into a single advertisement: "Guinness Time"; "Guinness is good for you" and "5 million enjoyed every day". The dancing ostrich was also used in animated television commercials.

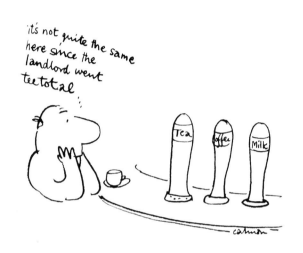

Give him a Guinness!

Press advertisement 1970

Agency J Walter Thompson
Artist M Calman

Calman's cartoon stands on its own, but is
given depth by the *Guinness* strapline.
The man's expression is truly doleful.

Press advertisement 1970

Agency J Walter Thompson
Artist M Calman

There is an acknowledgment of
Guinness' Irish heritage in one of
Calman's trademark faux-naïf
drawings for J Walter Thompson.

At the end of the day

The Introduction of Photography

As early as the 1930s, ground-breaking photomontage techniques had been applied to European advertising posters. The influential American Surrealist Man Ray had produced striking, enigmatic images on behalf of London Underground, while in Switzerland, graphic designer Herbert Matter's highly progressive posters for the Swiss Tourist Board demonstrated a harmonious synergy of photography and typography. Innovative as they may have been, these advertisements were minor aberrations, and illustration remained the dominant vehicle for printed advertising messages until the late 1950s. *Guinness* advertising was no exception, and John Gilroy was joined by a growing band of freelance illustrators and designers who continued to ply their trade through Bensons.

Press advertisement 1955

Agency SH Benson

By 1955 Bensons was starting to show both men and women drinkers in "realistic situations". A bottle of *Guinness* was still marketed as a drink with health-giving properties and messages such as "Guinness quickens the appetite" were the norm.

Press advertisement 1959

Agency SH Benson

Photography was used more and more in advertising towards the end of the 1950s, and by the mid-1960s it had become the preferred medium for most *Guinness* print advertisements.

But then the balance shifted irrevocably. This can, in part, be attributed to advances in printing technologies, but there was another, far more compelling reason. Bill Bernbach, founder of the New York advertising agency Doyle Dane Bernbach, is credited with instigating a "creative revolution", which changed not only the aesthetics of advertising, but also its day-to-day working methods. In *When Advertising Tried Harder*, a critique of American advertising in the 1960s, Larry Dobrow observes: "The look, the practices, the techniques of advertising that had been evolving for more than 60 years, were swept aside or radically altered by the power and excitement of the creative revolution. Illustration and strong graphics, which had long dominated the appearance of most advertising, were replaced almost totally by photography, which generated a completely different feel."

Art directors and copywriters were paired up for the first time, in order to enhance and enliven the relationship between words and images. The now-familiar press advertisement layout, with its well-defined hierarchy of photograph, headline and body copy was established. This was to become the basic advertising template for the next 30 years; indeed, it has only recently been challenged with the advent of the Apple Macintosh and the subsequent rise of post-modern design and typography.

In retrospect, this may seem a rather limited and formulaic means of constructing an advertisement, but at the time, the clarity of approach and simplicity of execution were truly radical. DDB's early portfolio, which included brilliant, incisive campaigns for Levy's Rye Bread, Volkswagen and Chivas Regal whisky, contains some of the greatest advertising of all time.

It must be remembered too, that within the new framework, there was still plenty of scope for well-crafted writing and expressive image-making. It also squared with Bernbach's assertion, that "our job is to kill the cleverness that makes us shine instead of the product. Our job is to simplify, tear away the unrelated, to pluck away the weeds that are smothering the product message." Bernbach's "revolution" swiftly arrived in Britain, and Bensons, along with the rest of its contemporaries, embraced it.

In fact, Bensons had already taken the plunge with photography as part of a black-and-white women's press campaign in the late 1950s and another which showed superimposed Gilroy animals "interviewing" people in photographs about their liking for *Guinness*. But the medium wasn't to become central to Guinness' creative strategy until the early 1960s.

The first few colour executions were little more than lovingly composed product shots; an empty bottle and a gleaming glass of beer with the words "Good for you" in red sans-serif capitals reversed out of a dark background. Slowly, embellishments began to appear: a tightly leaded, black "Good for you" headline above two full glasses of beer and a doctor's recommendation; in the same series, a bottle spied through an empty glass, with out-of-focus wallpaper in the background. A clear demarcation of the three elements (photograph, headline, copy) is becoming discernible, as the Bernbach model takes root.

This period also witnessed the introduction of the Hobbs-face, custom-designed by Bruce Hobbs, an art director at Bensons. Bristling with personality, it was based on stencil lettering and was characterised by

Press advertisement 1959

Agency SH Benson

Bensons' "Interview" press campaign had various superimposed Gilroy animals putting questions to people within photographs. Clearly a transitional campaign, it demonstrates Bensons' difficulty in embracing the emerging medium.

Press advertisement 1959

Agency SH Benson

The first television advertisements produced by Bensons featured both live and cartoon versions of John Gilroy's animals. The subsequent press advertisements went down the same route, using a combination of photography and cartoons.

wedge serifs and an abrupt contrast in the thick and thin strokes of the letterforms. Earlier versions have irregular, distressed edges, and are more angular in appearance than the slightly modified font which was introduced later. Hobbs is said to have derived his concept from the street signs of Paris and the crude lettering on hop sacks. He explained the rationale behind the design as follows: "I wanted to have something that had a feeling of authority about it, but at the same time had an elegance and was capable of being used in every conceivable way in which it might be required."

In 1990, the typeface was altered; renamed Design Group Hobbs, the new version was chunkier, but retained the stencil effect. Another variant, Hobbsian, was introduced in Ireland in 1997; leaner and more condensed than its predecessor, the break in the joins

GOOD FOR YOU

"In my opinion after thirty-seven years of general medical practice, Guinness stands high in the help which it can give to many patients. I order it very frequently after such debilitating conditions as influenza and other toxic conditions which leave so many people flat and lacking in energy. I also think that Guinness is indicated towards the end of a day which, in these hectic times, is often filled with strain and worry." M.B., Ch.B.

The Doctor who wrote this letter has given us special permission to publish it.

Press advertisement 1963

Agency SH Benson

This and the advertisement opposite hark back to the early campaigns of the 1930s, when *Guinness* stout was promoted for its health-giving qualities, and doctors' endorsements were incorporated into its advertising.

Press advertisement 1962

Agency SH Benson

The classic print advertising layout, comprising
headline, copy and boxed-off photograph,
emerged during the 1960s.

of the letter "N" is the only concession to its origins.
Initially the Hobbs-face was confined to advertising,
but in 1968 the typeface appeared on the *Guinness*
bottle label, and then was used on every conceivable
form of brand communication.

The combination of colour photography and the
Hobbs-face brought a totally new complexion to 1960s

Guinness advertising, and provided a platform for
several new campaign ideas. The first poster to
attempt to depict a true-to-life *Guinness* drinker, for
example, appeared in 1963, and was shot by the
celebrity photographer Terence Donovan. The accompanying headline read "Man! You've earned that
Guinness", harking back to the "reparative" campaign
of the 1950s, but suggesting a voguish 1960s patois in

its use of the word "Man!" as an exclamation. Another, more abstract, campaign from 1965 used a selection of evocative words such as "refresh", "good" and "deep" to put across *Guinness'* brand attributes.

In 1967, Bensons unveiled another approach, playing on the spatial relationship between the words and images. In one advertisement, the phrase "hold it" was placed inside the handle of a pint pot; in another, the word "plan" was by an overhead shot of a *Guinness* being poured into a glass, with the word "elevation" next to a side-on shot of a hand about to lift the full glass. The gentle punning anticipated the next major phase in *Guinness* advertising. But, ironically, this phase was the work of Guinness's new advertising agency, J Walter Thompson, rather than Bensons. □

REWARD !
YOU'VE EARNED THAT GUINNESS

Poster 1964

Agency SH Benson

The distinctive Hobbs-face was first used on a poster in autumn 1963. This particular example endorsed the idea of the "reparative" drinker.

Press advertisement 1965

Agency SH Benson

These were the first examples of *Guinness* advertisements designed to be shown in specific publications. By the 1990s this type of topical advertising had been taken a step further with the "Fractionals" and the "Black and White" campaigns: press advertisements that cleverly referred to real news stories on the same page.

Press advertisement 1965

Agency SH Benson

"Guinness for Scientists" was carried in the *New Scientist*. Other examples in the series were used in *The Listener*, the *Economist* and the *New Statesman*.

Poster 1965

Agency SH Benson

This poster shows another early example of the Hobbs typeface. Bruce Hobbs, an art director at Bensons, designed what he described as, "something that had authority about it, but that at the same time had an elegance and was capable of being used in every conceivable way." The predominant colours that Hobbs chose were all linked to *Guinness*: the black and cream to the drink's body and head and the red to its ruby gleam.

'What are you smiling about?'

'GU ESS!'

Poster 1966

Agency SH Benson
Design B Hobbs

It was almost inevitable that creatives would start playing around with the word "Guinness" itself. Bruce Hobbs' visual gag in this poster was to anticipate later campaigns such as "Guinnless" and "Genius".

Poster 1967

Agency SH Benson

The split-screen effect used in this poster took its cue from of one of the popular cinematic techniques of the era.

Plan

Elevation

Poster 1966

Agency SH Benson

This neat pun relied on the dynamic interplay of the visual and the verbal.

Poster 1967

Agency SH Benson

The first national campaign for Draught *Guinness* was launched in 1966. The distinctive Waterford tankard was adopted as the symbol for Draught *Guinness*, which replaced bottled *Guinness* as the physical manifestation of the product in mainstream advertising.

Displays and promotions

Guinness' core advertising campaigns have always been supported by what marketeers term "below-the-line" activity, in the form of special promotions and sponsorship. This is a well-established means of ensuring your brand name is never far from the minds of potential consumers, and is often managed by specialist consultancies rather than the frontline advertising agency.

In recent years, Guinness has launched intensive worldwide promotions in the run up to St Patrick's Day, March 17. In 1997, in the UK alone 17,500 on-trade promotions took place, with a phenomenal 9.5 million items of pub-based promotional material produced to support specially organised events such as "St Patrick's Party Nights" and competitions to win *Guinness* merchandise and trips to Dublin. Also in March 1997, Guinness sponsored the *Guinness* Village at the National Hunt Festival at Cheltenham and the *Guinness* Arkell Challenge Trophy Chase. The Manchester Irish Festival provides another suitable opportunity for building the *Guinness* brand through sponsorship.

The Irish Big Pint campaign of 1996 lent itself to impressive promotional events with giant, inflatable *Guinness* pints attracting considerable attention. A host of humorous promotional items themed around the Big Pint campaign included drinking mitts and hand strengtheners to enable customers to pick up their "Big Pint".

The current promotional programme has a lengthy heritage, in Britain and abroad, dating back to the Bensons' era. One of its earliest manifestations was the *Guinness* clocks, an extension of the "Guinness Time" poster campaign of the 1930s. There was a resplendent neon clock at London's Piccadilly Circus in 1929, as well as smaller clocks at busy railway stations including Lime Street Station in Liverpool and the Angel in Islington. They became popular landmarks, with friends arranging to meet "under the Guinness clock".

The most extravagant clock of all was the 25-foot-high "Guinness Festival Clock" created for the 1951 Festival Exhibition in Battersea Pleasure Gardens. This ornate musical timepiece, built by Baume & Co of

Window display 1950s

These types of displays
continued to be used
in Irish public houses
until quite recently.

Window display 1950s

This was an adaptation of the
"Guinness for Strength" campaign
for a Christmas promotion.

Window display 1950s

This window display mixed
2-D and 3-D *Guinness*
artefacts to create an enticing
visual tableau for passers-by.

Lorry tailboard 1954

Agency SH Benson

This was a mobile advertisement for *Guinness*. The toucan was a particularly popular device for vehicle liveries.

Lorry tailboard 1954

Agency SH Benson

The toucan took pride of place on a lorry tail-board in Kilmarnoch, Scotland.

Carnival float 1952

A *Guinness* strongman competition was held as part of a street carnival in pre-revolutionary Cuba.

In-pub display 1950s

Classic Bensons' posters were pasted over a local bar for a Nigerian special promotion.

Hatton Garden, was purported to be the most complex clock made in Britain for over 300 years. Every quarter of an hour, it burst into a frenzy of activity with a model of Gilroy's zookeeper ringing a bell; various doors then proceeded to open, revealing characters from *Guinness* advertisements, including a pair of toucans, the ostrich and the Mad Hatter.

In 1958, the clock was eclipsed by the opening of the *Guinness* Zoo in Great Yarmouth. Toucans, alligators, sea lions, pelicans, tortoises, kangaroos, kinkajous and brown bear cubs, as featured in Gilroy's advertisements, drew huge crowds to the Wellington Pier Gardens. In 1961, the *Guinness* Zoo moved on to Morecambe.

Such schemes were logical spin-offs from Guinness' mainstream advertising, as were the promotional enterprises in foreign markets. With the "Guinness for Strength/Power" campaign predominant, strong man competitions were held on a regular basis. Photographs from the Guinness archive show such events being held as part of a bustling carnival in pre-revolutionary Cuba in 1952, and in a more expected setting of a pub in the West Indies, also during the 1950s. A bulky competitor, stripped for action, is caught on camera

downing a bottle of *Guinness* as local children look on with fascination.

Pub and shop window displays, featuring bottles of *Guinness* together with posters, showcards and three-dimensional merchandise adapted from familiar advertising campaigns, were popular in Ireland until relatively recently. Liveried vehicles have provided another means of spreading the word: painted lorry tailgates, often featuring the *Guinness* toucan, were a common sight in Britain in the 1950s, while *Guinness* delivery vans could often be spotted in the busy streets of Far Eastern markets such as Malaysia and Singapore.

The *Guinness* 1954 "bottle drop" was another global, if somewhat random, means of promoting the beer abroad: using the company's shipping industry contacts, a large number of *Guinness* bottles containing a pseudo-parchment greeting and return address were dropped in the Atlantic, Pacific and Indian oceans. Recipients were asked to write back with details of when and where the bottle was found. Over 30 years later, replies were still coming in.

A more hi-tech manifestation of Guinness' below-the-line activities has been its foray on to the Internet and its downloadable PC screensaver.

**Guinness archives
1950s**

A promotional *Guinness* float made its way through the streets of Chicago.

Guinness archives 1950s

There was a regimented approach to point-of-purchase *Guinness* promotion in Japan.

Guinness archives 1960s

A fleet of *Guinness* mini vans, with bottles and leprechauns on their roofs, prepared to leave Liverpool on board a ship for the US where they were to be used in the New York area.

**Guinness archives
1950s**

A Malayan *Guinness* delivery van painted with the trade name of a local bottling company, Dog's Head.

**Guinness archives
1950s**

This photograph shows a competitor for the West Indian strong man competition testing the efficacy of the product.

Women drinkers

The 1970s was unquestionably a time when Guinness was trying to woo more women drinkers primarily through a J Walter Thompson campaign masterminded by the art director Ann Leworthy.

Lines such as, "Every girl should have a little black drink" and, "Why can't a woman be more like a man", were deliberately provocative, but the attached body copy contained cogent, hard-working argument. It maintained that *Guinness* was a boon to both sexes, and that as a woman, choosing

Press advertisement 1958

Agency SH Benson

Doe-eyed and deferential was how women in 1950s were portrayed in *Guinness* advertising.

'Thank you, Mike, for teaching me how good Guinness tastes!'

to drink it was to make a statement about one's individuality and independence.

The campaign also sought to position *Guinness* as a drink for the fashion-conscious, using "hot" photographers such as Barry Lategan and Harry Pecinotti to lend a fashion editorial feel to the advertisements. The combination of careful casting, make-up and hair contrive a perfect reflection of sophisticated 1970s chic.

Guinness can hardly be accused of resorting to using sex to sell. One mildly suggestive 1974 advertisement, however, showing a pair of tightly cropped red lips poised to take a sip out a of glass of *Guinness*, outraged Janice Winship of the Centre for Contemporary Cultural Studies at the University of Birmingham who claimed that "[the image] is a metaphor for the sexual act".

There were certainly far more overtly sexual advertisements around at the time including Smirnoff's risqué "The effect is shattering" campaign which pictured licentious scenes coupled with lines such as, "I thought the *Karma Sutra* was an Indian restaurant until I discovered Smirnoff".

In the *Guinness* press advertisement "Black goes with everything", a line-up of

Showcard 1954

Agency SH Benson

An illustrated showcard from the mid-1950s adopted a more fashion-conscious approach.

Press advertisement 1973

Agency J Walter Thompson

Photographer B Lategan

J Walter Thompson introduced a deliberately provocative press campaign aimed at women during the mid-1970s. Orchestrated by art director Ann Leworthy, it portrayed women as sassy and liberated, and used some of the top fashion photographers of the day.

Press advertisement 1973

Agency J Walter Thompson

Photographer H Pecinotti

This stylish press advertisement associated *Guinness* with fashion, but at the same time inferred that it rises above passing fads.

seven women are posed in a wide range of 1970s ensembles; the only thing they appear to have in common is that they're drinking *Guinness*. "Necklines rise and plunge", reads the copy. "Hemlines fall and rocket up again. Bottoms are in and out, bosoms come and go, colours wax and wane, waists move up and down then vanish and reappear. Only one thing remains constant and reliable.

And that's black." The text gently draws a parallel between fashionability and *Guinness*, but also implies that the drink somehow rises above it; black (and by inference *Guinness*) is described as "... good to look at. Restrained. Dramatic. At home in any company."

Admittedly, women featured in *Guinness* advertising hadn't always been so

Press advertisement 1974

Agency J Walter Thompson

Photographer B Lategan

A feminine, fashion advertorial feel moved
Guinness away from its traditional macho leanings.

Press advertisement 1974

Agency J Walter Thompson

Photographer B Lategan

This women's press advertisement used a bronzed bikini-clad
model to sell *Guinness*. The 1970s represented the emergence of a
new openness to sexuality particularly in magazines.

empowered. Witness the 1958 advertisement
in which a rather fragrant woman gazes at
her mentor (represented solely by the lower
portion of an arm and a glass of *Guinness*)
and exclaims gratefully, "Thank you, Mike,
for teaching me how good Guinness tastes".
But this representation – and others similar
– were essentially products of their era,
conforming to contemporary mores.

However, there are one or two examples
which show early *Guinness* advertising in a
progressive, almost liberated light: the

competent female factory worker in the
1961 "After Work" commercial, and a 1936
pen-and-ink press advertisement by John
Gilroy, which shows nine bowler-hatted
Underground commuters having to use the
stairs because the escalator is out of order
("Have a Guinness when you're tired", read
the posters on the wall). The second figure
up is an elegant bobbed-haired woman, who
is (perhaps) making her way to work.

* *Advertising in Women's Magazines 1956–74*

The inn drink

The Rise of the Pun

The influential Canadian cultural and media theorist Marshall McLuhan was scathing about British advertising, finding it "half-hearted and apologetic", in comparison to the more robust, direct approach of the Americans. "The Englishman," he proclaimed, "in his timid concern for demure good form, falls into the empirical bog of self-defensive puns, archness and snob-appeal."* The discrepancy in tone can, of course, be ascribed to cultural and historical differences, but it is significant that McLuhan homed in on the use of puns for particular censure.

Give him a Guinness!

Poster 1969

Agency J Walter Thompson

This poster lent a
comic twist
to the notion
of *Guinness*
as a reward.

He made this observation back in 1946, when a penchant for visual puns and trickery was much in evidence in British advertising. It wasn't until the early 1970s, however, that the verbal pun truly came of age. This coincided with, perhaps not surprisingly, a decision by Guinness to move its advertising account from SH Benson to J Walter Thompson. The newly appointed agency took full advantage of the now industry stock in-trades of "archness" and wordplay.

As a young copywriter, Chris Wilkins was drafted in to J Walter Thompson specifically to work on the Guinness account. He notes that at the time, "advertising was still a place where real writers went to get free coffee before the pubs opened; we were all serious graduates with aspirations to become serious writers". Showy, verbal gymnastics were the order of the day, as these would-be literati strove to impress each other and amuse themselves. Like Bensons, there was certainly a literary pedigree in the J Walter Thompson creative department of the era which, among others, included Dylan Thomas's son Llewellyn as well as Creative Director (and later Managing Director) Jeremy Bullmore, who had already enjoyed a distinguished career writing for radio.

Bullmore had originally been brought into the agency on the strength of his contribution to *Two Minute Theatre*, a popular radio show notable for its quickfire style. This experience, it was felt, should have prepared him for the demanding shorthand of television commercials. It was one of Bullmore's poster ideas from 1973 which unequivocally threw down the gauntlet to non-*Guinness* drinkers; it read (in quotation marks), "I've never tried it because I don't like it". The theme was later elaborated upon in

a television commercial in which a pub-goer is asked by his friend to partake in a blind tasting; on discovering he has been drinking *Guinness*, he announces incredulously, "But I don't like Guinness".

It was a brave, not to mention novel, strategy, questioning the assumption that the product must always be the hero of the piece, recognising that *Guinness* is an acquired taste, but highlighting judgmental, ill-informed attitudes. In some ways, it can be regarded as a forerunner to Ogilvy & Mather's "I hate Marmite" campaign of the mid-1990s, which used a similar though more extreme strategic idea to advertise another idiosyncratic product.

An earlier poster, "Are you afraid of the dark?" (1972), had used a similar line of reasoning, urging drinkers to at least give *Guinness* a try before writing it off. Others were more gratuitous in their use of wordplay, although you might argue that sharing a joke with potential customers is a legitimate, tried-and-tested ploy and continued *Guinness* advertising's long tradition of humour.

"Tall, dark and have some" (1972), "Red, white or black" (1972), which showed a glass of *Guinness* alongside glasses of red and white wine, and "A little dark refreshment" (1973), brought the product firmly into the equation. "The inn drink" (1971) and "Cool, calm and collect it" (1974), with a photograph of three pints of *Guinness* on a tray, were inventive enough, though less brand specific. "Hop squash", which pictured a jug of *Guinness* and a pair of long glasses on a rattan table in a sun-dappled garden, was too esoteric for its own good, and pilloried in *Campaign* magazine, the advertising industry's mouthpiece.

Give him a Guinness!

Poster 1970

Agency J Walter Thompson

The alliterative slogan and amusing
central image recalled the classic formula
established by Bensons.

The previous "Give him a Guinness" campaign, one of the earliest by J Walter Thompson, had featured posed photographs of hobbyists – a fisherman, gardener, DIY enthusiast – having completed a task, successfully or otherwise. Their reward for a job well done, or at least a brave effort, was a *Guinness*; the simple slogan, combined with an amusing image, echoed Bensons' well-worn formula. But as Thompson's got into its stride, the words became the focal point of *Guinness* poster advertising. The photography is proficient enough, but the images accompanying the series of pun-based advertisements are little more than

Press advertisement 1971

J Walter Thompson

The "Instant Guinness" advertisement, which provided detailed instructions on how to brew a pint of *Guinness* from a piece of newsprint, was published on April Fool's day.

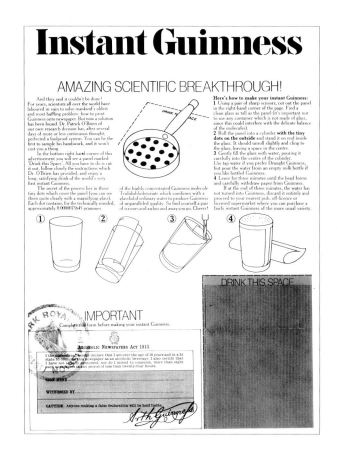

glorified pack shots. The Hobbs-face was temporarily discarded for a classic, no-nonsense Times, which further dampened the visual impact, allowing the words to work harder.

In *Watch This Space: Advertising Outdoors*, the former Creative Director David Bernstein writes: "...commonly a punning headline works at only one level. The intention is either to lure the viewer into thinking of one thing and then realising it refers to something else or to puzzle the viewer into making a connection between the brand and a seemingly unrelated message." J Walter Thompson's *Guinness* posters from the early to mid-1970s fully exploited both these aspects

of the punning headline – some more successfully than others. As Chris Wilkins candidly notes: "There are good puns and there are bad puns."

Press advertising gave J Walter Thompson the opportunity to be far more expansive. Often these immaculately crafted, perfectly judged advertisements took the form of elaborate hoaxes, such as the "Instant Guinness – amazing scientific breakthrough" advertisement from April 1, 1971, which gave detailed, step-by-step instructions on how to "brew" an instant *Guinness* by using a piece of blackened newsprint. "Use tap water if you prefer Draught Guinness, but pour the water from an empty milk

The inn drink.

Poster 1971

Agency J Walter Thompson

Guinness became synonymous with clever wordplay.

Red, white or black?

Poster 1972

Agency J Walter Thompson

This advertisement promoted *Guinness* as a meal-time drink.

Cool, calm and collect it.

Poster 1974

Agency J Walter Thompson

The use of the no-nonsense Times typeface dampened the overall visual impact and allowed the words to work harder.

bottle if you like bottled Guinness", ran the copy. In the "Special offer" advertisement from 1974, readers were urged to send off for "This unique and interesting beverage... finished in attractive black with contrasting white top", by filling in a coupon and enclosing a "cheque left obligingly open and made out to cash". Tick boxes for choices of colour were labelled black, black or black.

But it was undoubtedly television, which had by now become the dominant medium for advertising, at which Guinness' new agency excelled. Before long, Guinness had been established as a major force in the breaks between British television programmes. ☐

* American Advertising, reprinted from Horizon, October 1947.

Poster 1975

Agency J Walter Thompson
Photographer P Windsor

This was one of the most extra-vagant but least convincing puns of this era, ridiculed by *Campaign*.

Poster 1975

Agency J Walter Thompson
Artist J Cottrell

Thompson's highly literate copy-writers constantly strove to impress each other with their waggishness.

127

Poster 1976

Agency J Walter Thompson

The "It's as long as..." campaign of
the mid-1970s reintroduced a more
visual emphasis to *Guinness*
advertising.

Poster 1976

Agency J Walter Thompson
Photographer B Brown

This simple idea is charmingly
conveyed. The tall shadows
are well observed.

Poster 1976

Agency J Walter Thompson
Photographer T May

The snooker theme reappeared in the mid-1970s.
The black–and– white balls (*Guinness*) and the
green baize (Ireland) provided a strong visual analogy.

Poster 1978

Agency J Walter Thompson

Pub signs provided the framework for another
1970s poster campaign which highlighted
specific *Guinness* attributes.

'GUINNESS' is a Registered Trade Mark. GA/P32/2964

Poster 1978

Agency J Walter Thompson
Photographer T Copeland

Hijacking the visual iconography of the pub
was a logical way of appealing to pub-goers,
the primary consumers of *Guinness*.

Poster 1979

Agency J Walter Thompson

This abstract, wordless approach was undoubtedly influenced by Collett Dickenson Pearce's Benson & Hedges campaign which broke two years earlier.

Poster 1980

Agency J Walter Thompson

Photographer J Bantin

Enigmatic or just plain puzzling? The
swimming-pool suggested refreshment, but
the overall effect was slightly static.

Poster 1979

Agency J Walter Thompson

The draughtsboard with its black-and-white
squares was an obvious choice to help advertise
Guinness. It was to be re-used in the 1993
commercial, "Retreat", that featured Rutger Hauer.

Poster 1979

Agency J Walter Thompson
Photographer J Bantin

This was the least successful poster in the series.
Penguins may be black-and-white, but the
similarity with *Guinness* ends there.

The toucan

The *Guinness* toucan – probably *Guinness* advertising's most recognisable icon – began life as a pelican. In 1935, John Gilroy put together some initial sketches for Bensons' "Guinness a day" campaign featuring a pelican balancing seven pints of *Guinness* on its beak, together with this tentative copy:

A wonderful bird is the pelican,
Its bill can hold more than its belly can.
It can hold in its beak
Enough for a week:
I simply don't know how the hell he can.

Naturally enough, this rather clumsy verse was rejected, and copywriter Dorothy L Sayers – later to lampoon Bensons in one of her many crime novels, *Murder Must Advertise* – was asked to compose some new words. In doing so, she transformed the bird into a toucan. Her motives were purely pragmatic; the word "toucan" readily lending itself to the style of pun-laden copy she thrived on.

Gilroy developed the popular character to accompany Sayers' verse (page 48) from the tropical American fruit-eating bird with an immense beak, extravagant plumage and a penchant for mimicry. The toucan, who developed a more stylised, cartoon-like appearance in later incarnations, became a regular cast member of the Gilroy-orchestrated *Guinness* menagerie.

For over 25 years, it appeared on countless print advertisements, animated commercials, promotional merchandise and show cards, often sporting two pints of *Guinness* on its beak. A particularly classic toucan poster created by Gilroy in 1955 shows a pair of generously moustachioed RAF squadron leaders startled by five toucans flying in perfect formation overhead, each with a couple of pints on board (page 138).

When J Walter Thompson inherited the Guinness account in 1969, it was assumed that the days of the toucan were well over. Though the agenda of *Guinness* advertising remained essentially the same, Thompson's approach and remit were markedly different from Bensons. So when a "teaser" advertisement appeared in the advertising trade press in 1979, depicting a hatching egg with an orange and black beak emerging, many industry insiders felt it was a regressive step.

J Walter Thompson put forward a

Breaking soon, the new Guinness campaign.

Press advertisement 1979

Agency J Walter Thompson

Thompson's announced the long-awaited return of the toucan by taking a page in the *International Beverage News* in September 1979.

Poster 1979

Agency J Walter Thompson

The toucan was used in advertisements specifically designed to encourage sales of take-home *Guinness*.

Artwork 1955

Agency SH Benson

Artist J Gilroy

The *Guinness* toucan was often depicted with two pints balanced on its beak. This artwork, cut into four pieces for printing purposes, was later translated into an animated commercial.

Press advertisement 1981

Agency J Walter Thompson

The toucan provided a useful visual device for topical advertisements. This press advertisement appeared in the *TV Times* and marked the first British television screening of the Steven Spielberg blockbuster *Jaws*.

perfectly cogent argument for the toucan's revival. It was to front an entirely separate campaign for take-home sales, which would run in tandem with the principal campaign for draught sales. Thompson's also pointed out that the toucan was black–and–white, the colours being the very embodiment of a *Guinness*. The new toucan was photo-graphed using a combination of models and real birds and employed in a range of inventive topical press advertisements. The first television screening of the block-buster movie *Jaws* was marked by a toucan's beak gliding menacingly through shallow waters; the copy line read, "You could probably do with a Guinness tonight". A flock of toucans perched on the chimneys of familiar-looking slate roofs below the

Have you ever tasted a pint as good as Guinness?

Poster 1982

Agency J Walter Thompson

In print the toucan was represented photographically, to complement its live-action commercials.

headline "The Rovers Return" announced the screening of new toucan commercials in the advertisement breaks during the long-running soap opera *Coronation Street*.

The new series of toucan commercials proved remarkably popular. One of the finest portrayed a man attempting to prove to his friend that his toucan can talk. "What's this I'm drinking?" he asks. "Guinness," responds the bird. "What's John drinking?" he continues. "Guinness," replies the toucan. And so it goes on, with the toucan answering "Guinness" to every question. When the toucan's owner finally leaves the room, his friend asks it, "Who won the FA Cup in 1958?" The toucan

appears stumped. As his inquisitor rather smugly takes a sip of *Guinness*, however, it answers, "Bolton Wanderers".

Ironically, J Walter Thompson were finally to lose the Guinness account partly because of the public's enormous affection for the toucan. The popularity of the charismatic bird was detracting from the beer itself.

Guinness' new agency, Allen, Brady & Marsh, released a trade press advertisement showing chairmen Peter Marsh and Rod Allen balancing on a weather vane with the words "Lovely day for ABM". In homage to Gilroy's famous poster, they stood where the toucan had once been.

Poster 1981

Agency J Walter Thompson

The toucan was originally reinstated to encourage *Guinness* drinking at home, but became so popular that it eventually spearheaded the mainstream campaign too.

Poster 1982

Agency J Walter Thompson

This was the toucan's swansong and J Walter Thompson's last *Guinness* poster, which celebrated the birth of HRH Prince William of Wales in June 1982.

Television advertising

The Television Act of 1954 paved the way for the advent of commercial television in Britain, and the first advertisement break between scheduled programmes was duly broadcast on ITV at 8.12pm on 22 September 1955. It consisted of two 60-second commercials, one for Gibbs' SR Toothpaste, the other for Cadbury's Drinking Chocolate.

Despite a hefty 50 per cent premium above normal rates, many advertisers were determined to make an appearance on this auspicious evening. Guinness was no exception; its very first TV commercial was a brave attempt to bring John Gilroy's celebrated sea lion poster "to life", with the popular comedian Charlie Naughton playing the zoo-keeper and grappling valiantly with a temperamental sea lion hired for the shoot.

A crude effort by today's uncompromising standards, the sea lion commercial was fairly typical of the era. Uncomfortable with the new medium, advertising creatives tended to revert to the familiar, taking press or poster advertisements and "adapting" them for the small screen. The nation's very first commercial for Gibbs' SR Toothpaste was a case in point. It showed a tube of toothpaste and a block of ice as a voiceover recommended its "tingling fresh" qualities. This was a direct lift from an existing press advertisement, and just as static.

Similarly, the first Persil commercials were straightforward cartoon treatments of the washing powder's poster campaign, featuring dancers and sailors in different shades of white, with the sign-off line: "Persil washes whiter – that means cleaner". Bensons – almost inevitably – fell into the same trap with its first *Guinness* TV commercials, a series candidly titled "A Guinness poster come to life".

Many of these early films – for both television and cinema – used puppet animation produced by Joop Geesink, a Dutch studio. Others used cel animation by the highly regarded UK-based outfit Halas and Batchelor, best-known for its feature-length adaptation of George Orwell's political fable *Animal Farm* (1954), as well as commercials for Murray Mints and Daz washing powder.

Commercial 1953

Agency SH Benson
Studio Joop Geesink

Puppet animation was used in Joop Geesink's "Dollywood presents Weight and See".

Commercial 1958

Agency SH Benson
Production Company Screenspace

A cinema campaign called "The March of Progress" featured outlandish inventions and the catchphrase: "It's the more you drink it the more you like it drink".

Commercial 1957

Agency SH Benson
Studio Halas and Batchelor

A dancing toucans commercial entitled "Guinness Samba Time". The words of the music are variations on "Good for you" and "My goodness, my Guinness" set to a Latin American rhythm.

Guinness certainly had an extensive back-catalogue of material to plunder, and Halas and Batchelor's angular, contemporary style and technical ability could not be faulted. But treating a poster as a moment frozen in time and then manufacturing events before and after this "freeze-frame" brought mixed results. The beauty of Gilroy's originals was their economy and fluidity; they effortlessly suggested a past and a future. The way the "brought to life" commercials spelt it out for the audience verged on the heavy-handed.

A later, more original animated series, by the same studio, used Gilroy's zoo animals merely as a starting point, as they danced tangos, sambas and soft-shoe shuffles, with the zoo-keeper looking on approvingly.

Bensons' early attempts at live action commercials were equally hit-and-miss. A 1956 television campaign – which you can well imagine being mercilessly sent-up on a 1990s sketch show – featured a plummy bartender confiding that, "The chaps from the factory down the road like to drop in for a Guinness when they knock off. Wonderful how it bucks you up when you're tired." Not entirely surprisingly, it was redubbed with a more palatable accent for regions outside the home counties.

But one of the agency's less successful commercials attempted to animate the smiling "Guinness head", which for a time was used to sign off all *Guinness* commercials. A foam replica was painstakingly created by a model-maker; this sat on the top of a real glass winking mechanically, one of the least appetising representations of a pint of *Guinness* imaginable.

There were some welcome moments of light relief in the *Guinness* commercials of this period, however. An anarchic cinema campaign from the late 1950s showed a series of completely deranged inventions including a rocket-propelled bicycle, a "heli-hat" and the "Simkins Lunar Probe Mark One". None of them worked, of course, but after a *Guinness*, the crazed inventors could perform the desired feats anyway, without recourse to their contraptions. A television campaign aimed primarily at women, entitled "The Younger Generation", meanwhile, saw a line-up of young ladies expressing demure gratitude to their escorts for introducing them to the pleasures of *Guinness*: "You never said a truer word, Tom. Guinness does taste good." "Umm, you're right, George, Guinness does taste good."

It wasn't until the switch to the advertising agency J Walter Thompson in 1969 that *Guinness* television commercials began setting standards and winning significant creative awards. The ingenious "Ages of Man" commercial (1970) demonstrated human development through a series of drinks: a baby's bottle; a pint of milk; a fizzy soft drink; a glass of lager; and finally, a *Guinness*. The voiceover concludes, "It's good to grow up". Each stage was accompanied by a relevant sound effect: babies' gurgles, rugby songs, and so on, with gentle pub conversations representing *Guinness*, fully exploiting the twin facets of the medium.

Well-conceived pub-based comedy dialogue commercials became something of a *Guinness* staple in this period, featuring the kind of characters who'd be quite at home in the then-contemporary comedy series *The Likely Lads,* pondering the merits of a pint of *Guinness*.

In one such commercial, a flustered character rushes up to a man calmly drinking a *Guinness* and announces:

Commercial 1957

Agency SH Benson

This was part of the "Younger Generation" campaign that featured women drinkers. There were several versions with different regional accents.

Commercial 1959

Agency SH Benson

This extremely masculine campaign, aimed at blue-collar workers, showed trawlermen, crane drivers and steelworkers such as "Spud" Murphy (above), at work and enjoying a *Guinness* afterwards.

"...the Martians have landed at Stoke Newington and they're ravaging the whole countryside with their death rays." No response. "Macclesfield's been razed to the ground and the Greater London area has had to be evacuated. And the Isle of Man's sunk without a trace!" Still no response. Just then the barman calls: "Last orders, gents, please." "That's a pity," sighs the *Guinness* drinker.

1

2

3

4

5

Commercial 1970

Agency J Walter Thompson

The sophisticated "Seven Ages of Man" commercial showed an inevitable progression from a baby's bottle to a glass of *Guinness*, accompanied by suitable sound-effects. J Walter Thompson brought *Guinness'* commercials into the modern era.

Commercial 1976

Agency J Walter Thompson

"Phew!" used pub humour to put over the idea of drinking cold *Guinness* during the summer months.

Commercial 1980

Agency J Walter Thompson

An eminently catchy jingle contributed to the success of the "Barmaids of Britain" commercial.

Another commercial featured a pair of stereotypical young Frenchmen attempting to order *Guinness* in a pub. Try as they might, they simply can't pronounce the word "Guinness". A regular approaches the bar and asks for "the usual". "Two usuals," chime the quick-witted Frenchmen. The final shot shows them enjoying their drinks outside in the garden, eyeing up a woman as she passes by.

There was more domestic comedy too as the toucan, one of *Guinness'* most enduring symbols, was reintroduced in 1979.

One commercial showed a toucan sitting on a perch with a man standing in front of it repeating ad infinitum, "Don't forget the Guinness. Don't forget the Guinness." The toucan looks bemused.

Then the door opens, his wife comes in and the toucan says, "Bad news Mrs Harris.

Commercial 1973

Agency J Walter Thompson

Expanding on Jeremy Bullmore's "I've never tried it because I don't like it" poster, this commercial was centred around a blind-tasting in a pub.

Commercial 1981

Agency J Walter Thompson

"The Mechanic's Story", from the "Bottle of Guinness Supporters Club" campaign, saw J Walter Thompson adopting a more populist approach.

Your husband's turned into a parrot."

In 1976, the comedians Peter Cook and Dudley Moore were also brought in to front a campaign for take-home *Guinness*.

In less than 20 years, television advertising had developed beyond recognition and would continue evolving rapidly. In his book *The Best Thing on TV: Commercials* (1978), Jonathan Price underlined this point. "Culturally, commercials have trained our eye to accept fast cuts, dense and highly paced imagery, very brief scenes, connections that are implied but not spelled out – in brief, a new style of visual entertainment. Financially, commercials represent the pinnacle of our popular culture's artistic expression. More money per second goes into their making, more cash flows from their impact, more business thinking goes into each word than in any movie, opera, stage play, painting or videotape."

Commercial 1979

Agency J Walter Thompson

During the late 1970s, the toucan was used extensively in a drive to invigor-ate sales of take-home *Guinness*.

Commercial 1983

Agency Allen, Brady & Marsh

"Probe", a parody of TV documentary journalism, was one of seven commercials in Allen, Brady & Marsh's "Guinnless" campaign, which aired between 1983–1984.

Guinness is good for you

My goodness, my Guinness

Lovely day for a Guinness

At the end of the day

The inn drink

1983 - 1998 →

Guinnless isn't good for you

Pure Genius

Black and White

Guinnless isn't good for you

J Walter Thompson had good reason to be proud of its achievements during

its 13-year association with Guinness. The agency had swiftly reinvigorated

what had become a somewhat tired advertising programme during the final

months at Bensons, and its polished television work had added another

essential dimension to *Guinness* advertising.

Relief for the Guinnless

Issued by
Friends of the Guinnless

Poster 1983

Agency Allen, Brady & Marsh

The "Guinnless" campaign
was based on a double
negative proposition.

Though industry commentators questioned the wisdom of reintroducing the *Guinness* toucan in 1979, believing it to be a retrograde step, there was a sensible enough rationale behind the move. The toucan campaign was aimed specifically at take-home drinkers, and was quite distinct from the on-trade (pub) push. It was also extremely popular with the public; but perhaps too popular. It was even suggested at the time that the *Guinness* brand consisted of two discrete elements: *Guinness* stout and *Guinness* advertising, the latter having little effect on the former.

Guinness consumption figures seemed to bear out this theory. The decline in draught sales was particularly dramatic: volume fell by 38.5 per cent between 1972–1981 and the profile of the *Guinness* drinker aged noticeably. The time for polite, urbane advertising was over. Guinness moved its account to

Allen, Brady & Marsh, a brash young agency which had built a reputation for its aggressive, streetwise style. Allen, Brady & Marsh touted a form of "tabloid" advertising which purported to speak to the "common man". It was responsible for, among others, the National Milk Publicity Council's "Lotta Bottle", R White's "Secret Lemonade Drinker" and Guinness-owned Harp lager's "Harp stays sharp to the bottom of the glass" campaigns. It was the kind of insistent, irritatingly catchy advertising which managed to filter into popular culture, which people would quote at each other and satirists would see fit to parody.

Guinness withdrew from advertising for a full year before Allen, Brady & Marsh unveiled, with great fanfare, what it maintained was "the most thoroughly researched campaign in the history of British advertising". Chairman Peter Marsh had a well-known penchant for showmanship and hyperbole, but there was some substance behind his claim. Market statisticians, sociologists and psychologists were drafted in to complete exhaustive studies. Seven complete campaigns were prepared and tested; the one that finally ran was pre-tested at five stages of its development.

Allen, Brady & Marsh's campaign goals were demanding, consisting of a list of "musts": "the campaign must offer no confusion with any other beer; it must present Guinness more as a normal beer that might be enjoyed by anyone, but also a beer with a unique character; it must challenge the drinker to reassess his or her drinking habits; it must make Guinness 'top of the mind' and memorable and it must make it more approachable, a drink more 'for us' and less 'for them'." The campaign carefully targeted, in advertising industry language, at 24- to 34-year-old C2DE men. Research had revealed that this group represented as much as 71 per cent of all beer drinkers.

The first inkling of the new direction was a "teaser" poster which appeared in January 1983. It borrowed Bensons' familiar colour scheme: the green and black border and the red sans-serif type. But it showed an empty glass, together with the words "Guinnless isn't good for you", carefully reversing the original slogan. The poster, as intended, generated interest and bemusement in equal measure, before Guinness and Allen, Brady & Marsh revealed all to the media, licensees and city analysts during a spectacular four-day awareness programme conducted in a huge warehouse in London's Docklands.

Over 1000 people attended the launch which was staged by the design company Imagination. It was an all-singing, all-dancing affair, incorporating dramatic audio-visual and video displays and sound effects, in which the "story of Guinness" was brought to life, and the concept of "Guinnlessness" was revealed. It was a bravura stunt that typified Allen, Brady & Marsh's astute handling of the media. Public awareness of the new *Guinness* campaign continued to be perpetuated by newspaper column inches as much as the creative work itself.

Seven "Guinnless" commercials aired during 1983–84, all based on the problems of the "Guinnless", drinkers who had been without a *Guinness* for too long. The advertisements introduced The Friends of the

A word of comfort for the Guinnless

**Issued by
Friends of the Guinnless**

Poster 1983

Agency Allen, Brady & Marsh

The "Guinnless" were a group of unfortunates
who'd been without a *Guinness* for too long.

"Guinnless", a support group whose mission was to
help out these unfortunates, with each commercial
parodying a particular genre of television show.
"Revival", for example, spoofed a nature documentary,
as a David Attenborough-type stalked the "Guinnless"
on a beach; "Guinness Today" was a send-up of
hospital soap operas, showing a "Guinnless" patient
suffering from the condition "Monotonous pinticus".
Support material tended to show the product in pint
glasses and in a pub context, to make it accessible to
younger drinkers.

Within just three months of the £7 million campaign's
launch, it had achieved a phenomenal 87 per cent
spontaneous recall among British adults. A press
release claimed, "Clearly we have succeeded in
breaking the glass case of indifference. The campaign
is obviously achieving its aim – the repositioning of

155

Poster 1983

Agency Allen, Brady & Marsh

This "teaser" poster for the "Guinnless"
campaign used Bensons' graphic vocabulary.

Guinness as a more popular beer that everyone can
enjoy." In 12 months, the "Guinnless" campaign had
not only stopped the decline in sales of *Guinness*, but
actually increased it by 3.5 per cent.

Allen, Brady & Marsh's moment of triumph, however,
proved short-lived. Although the campaign was
deemed to have been a tactical success, it had serious
strategic short-comings. Basing a whole campaign
around a double negative proposition was short-
sighted and potentially confusing. Syntactical knots
were almost inevitable. For every person who
appreciated its humorous intent, there was another
who felt alienated by it. Apparently, the "Guinnless"
campaign was as annoying as it was memorable. The
portrayal of the "Guinnless" as disenfranchised misfits

Poster 1983

Agency Allen, Brady & Marsh

This seasonal adaptation of the "Guinnless"
theme has a typographic flavour.

also created an unfortunate image of the *Guinness*
drinker – what they inevitably became after they'd
undergone a "cure". Suddenly, there was a danger of
Guinness drinkers being portrayed in a negative light.

Findings from Allen, Brady & Marsh-commissioned
Cooper Research were the last straw. They stated that,
"Product attributes do not sell more Guinness... It is

by stating by what Guinness is not rather than what it
is that we have created and can develop this new
branding." This negative advice and rather churlish
sentiment rankled with the client, who had always
taken a justifiable pride in its product. It also totally
contradicted the long-standing credo of all *Guinness*
advertising – that the product itself should be central
to the creative strategy. □

Poster 1983

Agency Allen, Brady & Marsh

The "Guinnless" portrayed as the
Joker in a pack of playing cards.

Poster 1983

Agency Allen, Brady & Marsh

The extravagant cocktail anticipates Ogilvy & Mather's 1985 "Medallion Man" commercial.

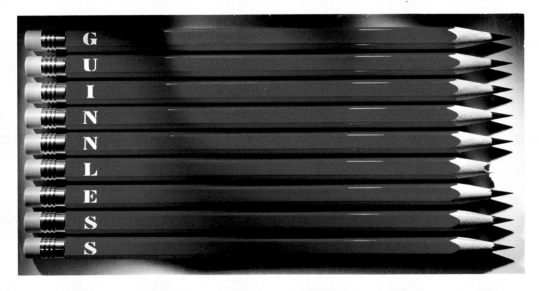

Poster 1983

Agency Allen, Brady & Marsh

This subtle advertisement refers back to the claim of *Guinness* as a tonic: it will sharpen you up.

Pure Genius

Symbolically at least, moving the Guinness advertising account to Ogilvy & Mather towards the end of 1984 was a return to its roots, the US-owned agency having bought out an ailing Bensons in the early 1970s. Ogilvy & Mather certainly seemed to have a thorough understanding of the Guinness heritage and the wherewithal to drive it forward into the next phase of consolidation, as became apparent during a fiercely contested pitch for the business involving six top London agencies.

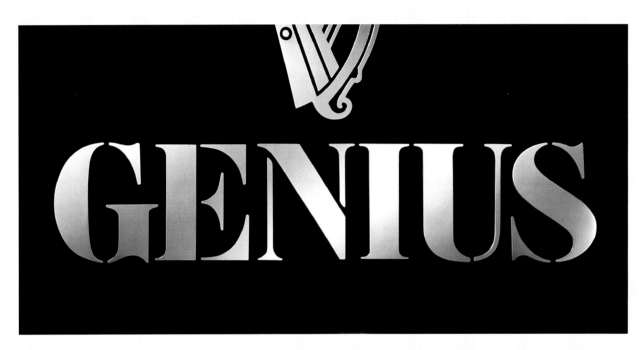

Poster 1985

Agency Ogilvy & Mather

The "teaser" poster which launched the
"Genius" campaign on 26 August 1985.

When Ogilvy & Mather's "Genius" campaign was
presented to the Guinness Chief Executive and
Marketing Department, they were so convinced of its
potential that they made their decision on the spot.
Famously, the concept had been conceived by
copywriter Mark Wnek, who had been holed up in the
Savoy Hotel with his art director Chris Monge with
instructions to stay there until they came up with a

winning campaign idea. At 1am on their third day in
the hotel, Wnek hurriedly scribbled something on a
piece of paper. It was the single word, "genius".

The beauty of the idea was that it could happily
embrace what had been isolated as the twin
objectives of *Guinness* advertising following a
comprehensive research programme conducted

during the summer of 1984. Firstly, to put across the values of the drink itself: that *Guinness* was mysterious, elemental, nourishing, rewarding and relaxing. Secondly, to articulate the image of the *Guinness* drinker in the pub: masculine, individual, independent and in control. The first represented the true reason people drank *Guinness*, while the second provided the "social permission" people needed to order a *Guinness* at the bar. The word "genius", of course, could apply equally to the drink or the drinker.

The new campaign was finally launched in August 1985 with a "teaser" poster consisting of the word "genius" and a harp half visible above it; this was closely followed by two extraordinarily lavish 60-second commercials directed by Nick Lewin.

The first, and more powerful of the two, titled "Natural Genius", was shot on location in Ireland and showed spectacular primeval scenes of earth, sun, fire and water, followed by clouds and wind passing over ripening corn, the corn being harvested and the stubble being burnt and the soil ploughed. The images conveyed a sense of the power and inevitability of nature and the ancient mysticism of Ireland, and implied that *Guinness* was the child of these powerful elemental forces.

"Natural Genius" and its sister commercial, "Power of Genius", which was similarly epic in intent, were designed to represent the brand's core values; two months later, they were joined by another pair of commercials aimed at projecting the profile of the *Guinness* drinker. According to John Wheelhouse,

Brands Director, GUINNESS, one effect of the *Guinness* campaign was to create somewhat of a "wally factor". This was seen to be detrimental and corrective measures were required.

The commercial "Armadillo" was set in an institute of sensory perception, with two men, separated by a screen, attempting to communicate using thought waves. As one visualises an object, the other sketches it on a pad of paper. The experiment is an unmitigated failure, until the scientist in charge tells his subjects they can't leave until they have "connected". Exasperated, the first man starts fantasising about a pint of *Guinness*. The second draws a rudimentary black pint on his pad. In the pub later, they are served a *Guinness* by a rather buxom barmaid. "Are you thinking what I'm thinking?" asks the first. "Armadillo," replies the second.

"Medallion Man" depicted a flashy wide-boy type, with a blonde woman draped on his arm, ordering a totally over-the-top cocktail in a wine bar. An elegant young man goes to the bar to order a *Guinness*, winning an admiring glance from the blonde.

The latter pair of commercials weren't quite as successful as the former, and were also perhaps a little too reminiscent of WCRS's Carling Black Label lager campaign, and others in a similar vein, which were in vogue at the time.

It became evident that running two separate campaigns for product values and user-imagery was too complicated. Both messages needed to be → p. 166

Press advertisement 1985

Agency Ogilvy & Mather

A combination of mystic symbolism and pub humour informed this early press advertisement from the "Genius" campaign.

Press advertisement 1985

Agency Ogilvy & Mather

The sophisticated art direction of the Genius campaign was a marked departure from the directness of the "Guinnless" campaign.

GUINNESS. PURE GENIUS.

Poster 1985

Agency Ogilvy & Mather
Illustrator N Broomfield

From the first burst of posters in the "Genius" campaign. "Darwin" was later slightly adapted and used as part of a Russian advertising campaign.

Poster 1985

Agency Ogilvy & Mather
Photographer J Oke

Here Guinness continued
the tradition of making
an old joke its own.

Poster 1985

Agency Ogilvy & Mather
Photographer J Oke

The cryptic tone of "The
Man with the Guinness"
began to emerge.

THE HEAD OF BRITISH INTELLIGENCE

GUINNESS. PURE GENIUS.

Poster 1985

Agency Ogilvy & Mather
Photographer J Oke

This was from the second batch of "Genius" posters released in the latter part of 1985.

THOUGHT PROCESS

GUINNESS. PURE GENIUS.

Bus side poster 1987

Agency Ogilvy & Mather

This is a creditable application of campaign idea to media. The sense of anticipation is almost palpable as the glass gradually fills up over seven shots. There is a faint echo of J Walter Thompson's "Pint sighs" poster (page 127).

incorporated into a single campaign. The "Genius" poster campaign, however, didn't suffer from such schizophrenia. "Darwin", illustrated by Nick Broomfield, tampered with the classic classroom diagram showing the various stages in human evolution from ape to Homo sapiens, with the final figure a huge pint of *Guinness*. "The Australian for Genius", photographed by Jerry Oke, pictured a pint of *Guinness*, with its distinctive white head anchored to the bottom of the glass. "Thought processes" was a long, landscape poster designed for bus sides that

showed 13 successive shots of a glass of *Guinness* being gradually filled and then emptied.

The press advertisements followed a similarly intriguing route. They were designed to draw in the viewer and create a sense of involvement; there was reward (in the form of amusement) to be had if he or she bothered to do so, mirroring the benefits of acquiring a taste for *Guinness*. Their polished art direction was in marked contrast to Allen, Brady & Marsh's no-frills approach.

Poster 1987

Agency Ogilvy & Mather

This pun harks
back to SH Bensons'
"Alice in Wonderland"
advertisements.

Poster 1987

Agency Ogilvy & Mather

The "Snow Venus de
Milo" poster was first
used in Ireland to
promote *Guinness* as
a cold drink.

The campaign's versatility was evident in some of the below-the-line activities it generated, such as the "Genius poll", which attempted to discover who the British public thought was Britain's greatest ever genius (Sir Winston Churchill), the greatest unsung genius (Bob Geldof) and the greatest living genius (Sir Clive Sinclair). In contrast to Allen, Brady & Marsh's "Guinnless" campaign, it was clear that Ogilvy & Mather's "Genius" campaign had legs. But as yet, it hadn't quite found its feet. □

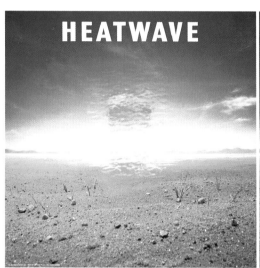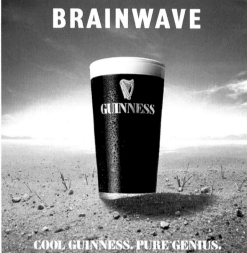

Poster 1987

Agency Ogilvy & Mather

The core campaign message and a specific strategic message were conveyed in this single poster.

Poster 1987

Agency Ogilvy & Mather

This well-executed abstract image owes a debt to Collett, Dickenson & Pearce's Benson & Hedges campaign.

Poster 1987

Agency Ogilvy & Mather

The "Summer Cool" campaign became a regular fixture, but now the words "Pure Genius" were added.

Poster 1985

Agency Ogilvy & Mather

Another diptych approach was used to encourage the consumption of cold *Guinness.*

169

Commercial 1985

Agency Ogilvy & Mather

Director N Lewin

"Natural Genius" was shot on location in Ireland and represented the natural goodness of *Guinness* through potent images of earth, sun, fire and water. Its rich textures and primeval grandeur set it apart from the more parochial efforts of the competition.

4

5

6

Commercial 1985

Agency Ogilvy & Mather
Director N Lewin

Similarly epic in intent, "Power of Genius" presented a mysterious science-fiction world, with *Guinness* as a powerful regenerative force. Shot at Pinewood studios, with lavish sets created by Brian Etwell, it showed a *Guinness* being spilled and apparently causing a power cut. As the glass is refilled, the lights come back on and the community comes back to life.

4

5

Worldwide advertising

Guinness is a truly global brand, easily the best-selling stout in the world. From the very early days of its history, it was widely exported from Dublin; today it is brewed in 51 markets and sold in over 150, with major overseas markets in West Africa, the Far East and the Caribbean.

Advertising strategy tends to be driven by the needs and idiosyncrasies of local territories, advised and supported by the central marketing resource, Guinness Centre Marketing, based at the Park Royal Brewery in London. London tends to take the lead on matters of brand positioning, product strategy and packaging development, while the regions and markets direct local advertising.

There is no global advertising strategy or agency network as such, with each market responsible for establishing its own agency links: these include Weiss Whitten Stagliano in the US, Globespan in Africa, and Ogilvy & Mather in Asia-Pacific.

Market research has shown that *Guinness'* product values are essentially the same across the major markets as regard to appearance, taste and benefits. Advertising has followed a broad model across the globe, different stages being reached by different markets at different times.

The first stage of the model is that "Guinness is good for you", expressed overtly, through the representation of physical benefits. This is followed by the same message articulated covertly, stressing its mental benefits. Finally, when the market is ready, vaguer concepts such as personal satisfaction are introduced.

The various territories may be culturally and demographically diverse, but there are some discernible recurring themes which have been used in *Guinness* advertising throughout the world. The most prominent is undoubtedly the restorative/replenishment theme – similar to that employed in Britain during the late 1950s to mid-1960s. In the Far East, a popular, long-running endline was, "Guinness puts back what the day takes out", building on previous "Guinness for Strength" and "Guinness for Power" campaigns. Recently, however, the emphasis has become more sophisticated and aspirational, shifting away from the original base of manual workers.

Showcard 1950

Agency SH Benson
Artist J Gilroy

The cartoon-like
Guinness head was
put to work in Italy
with a different
message.

Showcard 1949

Agency SH Benson
Artist J Gilroy

This advertisement
showed a
straightforward
adaptation of
a Gilroy poster
produced for the
French market.

A similar thread is apparent in West Africa, though the three-stage model has been slower to develop. A Nigerian "Guinness for Power" poster from 1962 shows a Nigerian lumberjack, having sawn through a huge tree trunk, skipping away with it on his shoulder, echoing the celebrated "girder" poster.

Almost 20 years later, a photographic poster from the Cameroon targets a similar audience with a similar message, using a smiling, hard-hatted worker holding a glass of *Guinness* while the French wording reads

"Découvrez la force" ("Discover the power").

Cameroon posters still associated *Guinness* with strength in the 1990s, albeit slanted towards athleticism, in a poster showing a javelin thrower and the single word "Puissance"; the art direction is slicker and the model more refined than earlier campaigns. A Nigerian poster campaign, meanwhile, adopted a complex triptych approach, with images representing the words "Stronger. Richer. Smoother".

Over the years, certain unaccountable myths have developed in parts of the world → p. 178

Press advertisement 1964

Agency SH Benson

A Gaelic touch was added to a simple black-and-white line-drawn press advertisement by Bensons.

Showcard 1961

Agency SH Benson
Artist J Gilroy

The seaside theme, as used in John Gilroy's final British poster, was deemed an appropriate subject for a Channel Islands pub showcard.

Poster 1950s

Agency SH Benson
Artist J Gilroy

Natural goodness
was highlighted in
this 1950s Russian
poster.

Poster 1990

Agency Rawlins Wickens Partnership

Guinness' traditional link with strength was
retained in this advertisement, but the bias
shifted towards athleticism, in a poster which
ran in the Cameroon and the Ivory Coast.

Enamel sign 1968

Agency Lintas

The glass of *Guinness* appeared to be talking in
an illustrated poster from the Cameroon,
which conveyed one of the earliest advertising
messages: "Guinness does you good".

about the powers of *Guinness*, most notably
that it "feeds the blood", and is a powerful
aphrodisiac. This property is hinted at
obliquely in various local campaigns,
particularly in Africa and the Caribbean. An
ambiguous 1992 poster from the West Indies
shows a bikini-clad woman standing on a
beach. In the foreground two hands, each
holding a glass of *Guinness*, are positioned
directly under her breasts. It's not clear
whether she is being approached by a friend

bearing drinks or perhaps being toasted by
two men and the suggestiveness is
heightened by the word "Satisfying".

In Europe, where advertising can afford
to be more oblique, one of the most innovative and refreshing *Guinness* campaigns of
recent years emerged in Spain during the
late 1980s. The "Guinness La Otra Cerveza"
("Guinness, the other beer") campaign was
developed for both television and press,
depicting *Guinness* as a black spot in a series

Poster 1970s

Agency Ammarati Puris/Lintas

Guinness' Caribbean campaigns often featured images of women.

Poster 1992

Agency Rawlins & Wickens Partnership

This was a more obviously suggestive poster from the Caribbean. The positioning of the glasses heightened the innuendo of the headline.

of tableaux. "Red Square" showed a black spot on a red background; "Where is my Guinness?" was a black page; "Association of Guinness Drinkers", a cluster of black spots.

In the United States, all-time great practitioners such as David Ogilvy have worked on Guinness' behalf; indeed the market has achieved such levels of consumer sophistication that the international advertising model no longer applies.

Part of *Guinness'* popularity in the US

can probably be attributed to the high number of Irish immigrants that have settled there, particularly in New York, and who are still faithful to the brand. Most of the earliest advertising campaigns from the mid-1930s, following the repeal of prohibition, were targeted at the Irish audience and concentrated on the brand's Irish roots through the archetypal symbolism of leprechauns and shamrocks.

While the early US advertisements did

not follow the typographical style created for *Guinness* by Bensons, they did borrow key elements from the UK agency. The smiling *Guinness* pint face, created by John Gilroy in the 1930s, remained an important feature in US advertisements twenty years later as did the popular "Guinness for strength" theme. One such press advertisement from 1953 (Compton Advertising) showed a grinning man throwing an enormous moose to the ground with ease while the advertisement read: "Now enjoy flavor twice as strong as beer."

The advertising agency Weiss, Whitten & Stagliano introduced more universal humour to the US poster campaign in 1993, showing characters in intensely satisfying poses – a man lying back having a manicure and pedicure, being offered lobster, smoking a cigar, and enjoying a violin recital all at once – with the strapline: "Almost as satisfying as a Guinness".

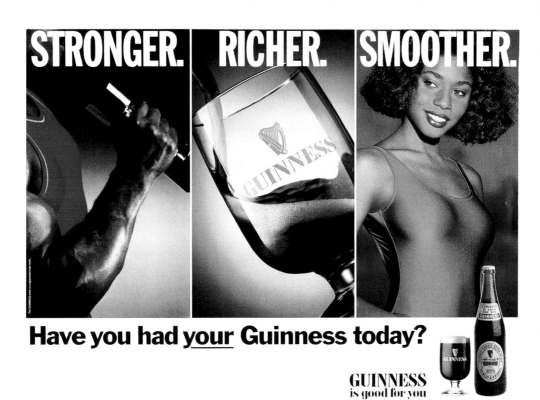

STRONGER. RICHER. SMOOTHER.

Have you had <u>your</u> Guinness today?

GUINNESS
is good for you

Poster 1992

Agency Rawlins & Wickens Partnership

A photographic triptych allowed three aspects of *Guinness* to be projected on a more recent Nigerian poster.

A more recent Weiss, Whitten & Stagliano television campaign launched in October 1996 and titled "Senses" aimed to expand *Guinness* drinkers beyond the regular drinkers to include new recruits and occasional "triers". The award-winning campaign focused on the ritual of drinking *Guinness* and explored this as a rich sensory experience. The advertisements conclude with the copy line "The perfect pint".

With the quality and sophistication of advertising techniques on the increase throughout the world, the "reparative" theme has been superseded by a more subtle aspirational style. Guinness has made a point of tapping into the culture and social mores of individual territories and communicating its core values within an appropriate context. As varied as the results may be, *Guinness* advertising remains a fascinating reflection of the many societies it serves.

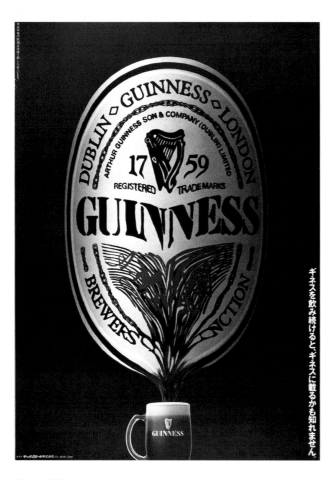

Poster 1989

Agency Ogilvy & Mather

This poster represents an unusually graphic approach from Japan, with the label dissolving into the glass.

Poster 1960s

Agency Lintas

A colourful, illustrated man-with-pint approach, reminiscent of movie posters of the era, was used in Malaysia. *Guinness* was unequivocally known as *Guinness* Stout in the region.

Poster 1993

Agency Mark Design

Malaysia is divided into three areas: Peninsula, Sabah and Sarawak. Guinness has made use of separate advertising campaigns to reflect the ethnic and cultural differences between them.

Poster 1993

Agency Mark Design

The model above wears traditional costume appropriate for Sarawak, while in the adjacent poster, the model wears western clothes suitable for the Peninsula region. Different shaped bottles are used in the two areas.

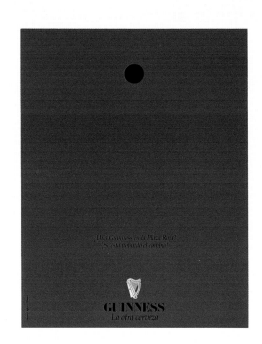

Asociación de amigos de Guinness.

GUINNESS
La otra cerveza

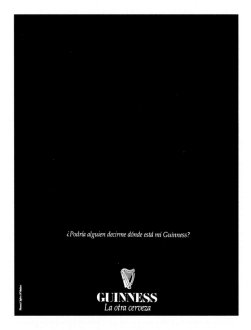

¿Podría alguien decirme dónde está mi Guinness?

GUINNESS
La otra cerveza

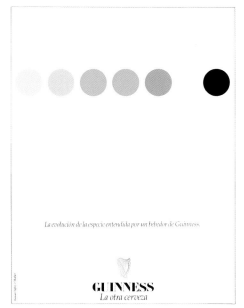

La evolución de la especie entendida por un bebedor de Guinness.

GUINNESS
La otra cerveza

Press advertisements 1989

Agency Ogilvy & Mather

When it was launched, the "Black Spot" campaign was hailed as the "most original campaign ever made in Spain". Its aim was to highlight the brand's individuality.

Poster 1995
*Agency Ammarati
Puris/Lintas*

The Canadian "It's not
beer. It's stout" campaign
used the *Guinness* bottle
itself as metaphor for
strength.

Poster 1995
*Agency Ammarati
Puris/Lintas*

Both strength and
individuality were
articulated in the
Canadian campaign. The
unusually long format lent
further visual impact.

Press advertisement 1989
Agency Ogilvy & Mather

The Belgian "Contrasts"
campaign appealed to
connoisseurs and younger
drinkers.

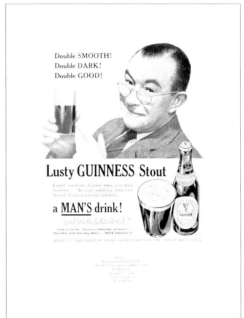

Press advertisement 1950

Hewitt, Ogilvy, Benson & Mather

Guinness advertisements of the 1950s in the US, this one pointedly aimed at men, used the smiling pint glass as a consistent sign-off motif.

Press advertisement 1953

Compton Advertising

One of Bensons' campaign themes, "Guinness is strength", made a comeback in this advertisement along with the smiling pint glass and a character reminiscent of John Gilroy's flat-capped zoo keeper.

Press advertisement 1950

Hewitt, Ogilvy, Benson & Mather

Early *Guinness* advertisements in the US drew attention to the drink's Irish heritage and the large number of Irish immigrants in the country.

Poster 1993

Agency Weiss, Whitten & Stagliano

A series of intensely "satisfying" scenarios were contrived in this comic US campaign.

Poster 1993

Agency Weiss, Whitten & Stagliano

The retro styling of the "Almost as satisfying..." campaign hinted at *Guinness'* pedigree.

Commercial 1996

Agency Weiss, Whitten & Stagliano

The "Senses" campaign approached drinking *Guinness* as a sensory experience. "The nod, the cascade, the wait, the first sip: why every man has five senses."

Commerical 1996

Agency Weiss, Whitten & Stagliano

Also part of the "Senses" campaign, this one called "Dream" asked: "Do you dream in black-and-white?" ending with the campaign's sign-off: "The perfect pint".

The Man with the Guinness

Following the mixed reception of the "Pure Genius" campaign,

Ogilvy & Mather quickly realised it required a cipher potent enough to

signify *Guinness'* product values and user imagery simultaneously.

Some sort of spokesperson seemed the most logical route.

But what kind of spokesperson exactly?

Illustration 1794

This early illustration from the pages of *The Gentleman's Magazine* could be one of the first representations of the *Guinness* drink.

PORTER.

HEALTH, PEACE AND PROSPERITY
An eighteenth century view of the virtues of Porter

35

Commercial 1993
Agency Ogilvy & Mather
Director Hugh Hudson

The Dutch-born actor Rutger Hauer became a "walking piece of brand identity" for *Guinness* in the late 1980s. At its height, awareness of the campaign was double that of most other beers.

189

There were several false starts before "The Man with the Guinness" emerged. A complex amalgam of signifiers, he was to resemble *Guinness* both physically (in that he was broad shouldered, dressed in black, with a smooth, blond head) and psychologically (being robust, enigmatic and deep). "The Man with the Guinness" was also intended to emphasise individuality, a key buzzword during the mid-1980s. This was the height of the Thatcher era; when all the signals were that the British economy was booming and a climate of aspiration and self-reliance prevailed.

Advertising, which had by now become a highly sensitive cultural barometer, reflected the mood. The British director Ridley Scott shot a lavish commercial for Apple Computers which took its cue from George Orwell's political novel *Nineteen Eighty-Four*. It showed a woman racing into an auditorium of faceless, boiler-suited workers mesmerised by a massive talking head bellowing from a screen ahead of them. She swings a huge hammer above her head, flinging it towards the screen just as a posse of guards are upon her. The message was clear: Apple was the choice of the colourful individual, not the monochrome masses.

Guinness wanted to take the notion of "individualism" a stage further: "We asked ourselves what does 'individualism' actually mean?" explains John Wheelhouse, Brands Director, GUINNESS. "We needed a character who was strong, attractive and confident, someone who was a source of wisdom yet still streetwise. It couldn't be just a veneer, he had to have a texture and depth appropriate to Guinness, which linked back to the product."

Fosters lager was one of the beers at the time which used a character to represent the brand. Appropriately enough, it employed quintessentially Australian actor Paul Hogan, star of the *Crocodile Dundee* films, as a frontman. But Hogan had a tendency to overpower the brand. As Wheelhouse puts it, "there was a danger of the Fosters campaign becoming the Paul Hogan Show". It was a pitfall Guinness was determined to avoid.

The casting process was lengthy, but the final choice was inspired. Rutger Hauer was a Dutch-born actor with a cult following, best-known for his portrayal of a highly sophisticated killer "replicant" in the sci-fi movie *Bladerunner*. He wasn't well-known enough in Britain for his presence in the commercials to constitute an endorsement, but his face would have been vaguely familiar, especially to the film-going cognoscenti.

The campaign was launched in May 1987 with the first commercial, "Mars". "The Man with the Guinness" is shown in a series of surreal environments, ending up in a chintzy armchair in the middle of Hyde Park, with a pint of *Guinness* in his hand. The script ran, "The planet Mars is paradise. Voices are never raised in argument. Never. There's only one sex; so, no emotional problems. No fast cars or noisy discos. Every one is equal and lives to 803. Me, I sold up and moved to Earth."

The next commercials built on the first, reinforcing the connection between the man, his circumstances, his *Guinness* and the viewer. They had a compelling intensity, reflecting their role as "a modern parable

Press advertisement 1987

Agency Ogilvy & Mather

"Teaser" advertisements hinted at what
was to follow in the MWTG campaign.

Commercial 1987
Agency Ogilvy & Mather
Director Barney Edwards

"If it didn't exist, you'd have to invent it." Ten-second commercials, such as "Dinosaur", were the "yeast which leavened the bread" of the longer advertisements.

"If it didn't exist, you'd have to invent it"

worth decoding". Before long, "The Man with the Guinness" had become an established advertising icon, dispensing such puzzling pearls as, "It's not easy being a dolphin", and "On the subject of colour, I'm with Henry Ford. Okay?"

Five months after the campaign's launch, a Draught *Guinness* brand review declared, "The Man with the Guinness campaign has successfully met the objective of establishing the individualism of Draft Guinness in a way which links the drink and the drinker... the

campaign has the potential to run for a long time, perhaps even one which will be recognised as a classic campaign, certainly one which upholds and develops the Guinness advertising tradition."
The campaign's impact was undeniable; but it was so radical and different from what had gone before and the competition's offerings that it initially polarised opinion.

Bylined as "the copywriter on Ogilvy & Mather's controversial current Guinness campaign", Mark Wnek

"It's not easy being a dolphin."

Commercial 1987
Agency Ogilvy & Mather
Director Barney Edwards

"It's not easy being a dolphin." The effectiveness
of the first Rutger Hauer commercials was based
on a mixture of simplicity, style and strangeness.

launched a staunch defence of his work in the
November 1987 issue of creative magazine *Direction*:
"[the campaign] seeks to hang on to the impact,
originality and intrigue of the past while communicating to today's market. It seeks to draw new
consumers into the fold, people who weren't around in
the Good Old Days, people who, even if they recall the
great Guinness ads of the past, find them dowdy,
daunting and irrelevant. The latest Guinness campaign
makes no concessions whatsoever that Guinness is a
difficult drink to get into, a hard taste to acquire. The

question is: is Guinness, as portrayed in the new
advertising, a taste worth acquiring?"

The answer was a resounding yes. By 1991, with the
campaign still going strong, Draught *Guinness* had
enjoyed five years of consistent growth. *Guinness*
sales, along with the previously stagnant black beer
market, had been totally revitalised, though there were
other contributing factors involved in this upsurge in
its fortunes, including an increase in distribution and
the advent of Draught *Guinness* in a can.

Commercial 1990
Agency Ogilvy & Mather
Director Paul Weiland

"Funny" drew attention to the creamy *Guinness* head, as well as developing the MWTG's personality by having him poking fun at himself.

"I've been accused of taking myself too seriously... Not guilty."

Commercial 1990
Agency Ogilvy & Mather
Director Paul Weiland

Two versions of "Telepathy" were produced. One ended in silence after the MWTG informed us we'd hear something if we were telepathic, the other with the words, "I've lost Horace, my teddy bear. If you see him, please send him home."

"I have a secret; but I'm a little shy, and I can't just tell anyone; so you'll only hear it if you're telepathic... Thank you for listening."

Commercial 1991

Agency Ogilvy & Mather
Director Ridley Scott

"Dark Glasses" was one of
five advertisements shot by
the director of *Bladerunner*
and *Alien*.

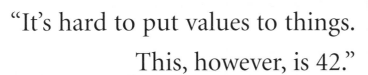

"Blue skies. Blazing sun. Solution: dark glasses."

Commercial 1991

Agency Ogilvy & Mather
Director Ridley Scott

"Games", also known as "Games Room",
was set in a stately room with board games,
a can of *Guinness* and a pint on a table and
was one of the more obscure offerings
from the long-running campaign.

"It's hard to put values to things.
This, however, is 42."

A succession of top-flight commercials directors –
Barry Kinsman, Paul Weiland, Hugh Hudson and Ridley
Scott – steered "The Man with the Guinness" through
his surreal odyssey, some advertisements
representing a general fixation with *Guinness*, others
specific product attributes such as drinking it cold
("Chilly, isn't it?") or Draught *Guinness* in cans ("My
brother and I are identical in every way. Except you can
take me anywhere."). The character's conundrums
became ever more obscure, but latterly the viewer had
come to expect and enjoy the challenge. Stylistically
the campaign developed too, moving away from the

"On the subject of colour, I'm with Henry Ford. Okay?"

Commercial 1991
Agency Ogilvy & Mather
Director Ridley Scott

"Henry Ford" was shot in black-and-white and showed the MWTG, in a dressing gown, getting his *Guinness* from a wood-panelled fridge.

Commercial 1991
Agency Ogilvy & Mather
Director Ridley Scott

The MWTG strolls through works of art by Frans Hals, Van Gogh and Renoir (left) before asking: "Get the picture?"

"Get the picture?"

Commercial 1993
Agency Ogilvy & Mather
Director Hugh Hudson

The last few commercials, such as "Retreat", became more and more extravagant, as the campaign finally ran out of steam.

"If you keep an open mind, you'll discover dark secrets ?"

"talking head" format to a more ambitious journey into the mysteries of *Guinness* with the Hauer character as an interpreter.

Working in tandem with the television work was a simple but highly effective press campaign (occasionally extended to posters and adshels) created by Ogilvy & Mather art director Brian Fraser,

known as "Fractionals". These naïve, black-and-white doodle-like drawings ran from March 1991 to 1996, purporting to be the absent-minded jottings of "The Man with the Guinness". Often they were topical, referring to specific occasions such as the Wimbledon Tennis Championships or St Patrick's Day, others placed a drawing of a pint of *Guinness* in a background such as a bar code ("Subliminal

Commercial 1990

Agency Ogilvy & Mather

George Lam became the MWTG in
Singapore. Commercials were shot in
Mandarin, Cantonese and English and
based on well-known Chinese proverbs.

Advertising"), or musical bars ("Smooth tempo").
"The Man with the Guinness" campaign was used
extensively abroad, though in several territories Hauer
was replaced by actors more appropriate to local
markets. In Australia, Wenanty Nosul, at that time a
relatively unknown actor and "a little rougher round
the edges" than Hauer, was drafted in for a campaign
which ran from 1989–1993. In just three months sales
had jumped by 22 per cent. In Singapore and Hong
Kong, well-established actor George Lam took the part
in a campaign centring around Chinese proverbs, with
the endline "Guinness – a word of wisdom", shot in
Cantonese, Mandarin and English. Within two years,
consumer awareness was running at 91 per cent. New
Zealand was the only country outside Great Britain
where the Rutger Hauer commercials were used.

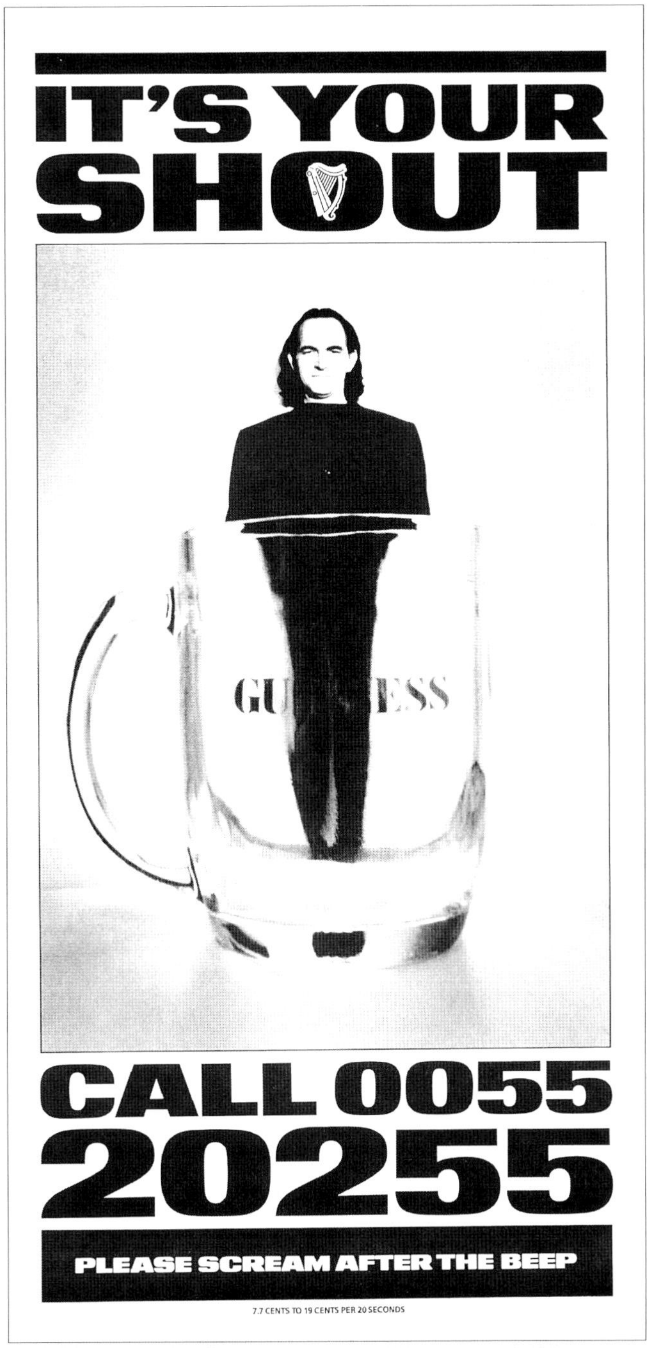
IT'S YOUR
SHOUT
GUINNESS
CALL 0055
20255
PLEASE SCREAM AFTER THE BEEP
7.7 CENTS TO 19 CENTS PER 20 SECONDS

Press advertisement c 1990
Agency Ogilvy & Mather, Sydney
Wenanty Nosul became the MWTG in Australia, where sales jumped 22 per cent in three months after the campaign was launched.

Commercial 1994

Agency Ogilvy & Mather

"Chain" represented a surreal journey into the heart of a pint of *Guinness* and back out again.

1

The last glimpse of "The Man with the Guinness" was a flickering image on a black-and-white television during the commercial "Chain".

2

"The Man with the Guinness" series aired for eight years, a remarkable run for a modern campaign. However, by the early 1990s, several rival beer brands had latched on to the formula and were using eccentric spokespeople talking directly to the camera to advertise their products; GGT Advertising's Holsten Pils campaign, with the actor Jeff Goldblum, was particularly similar in tone. This, of course, diluted *Guinness'* distinctiveness. "The campaign had reached a plateau," says Tom Bury, Deputy Chairman of Ogilvy & Mather. "Some did better than others, but the over-all feeling was that it was getting a bit old and tired."

The room set in "Chain" contained several visual references to *Guinness* iconography and to previous advertisements. Note the harp, the teddy bear, the picture frames and the diver's helmet.

3

4

This "Chain" commercial placed, in the very centre of the room, next to a book on Chaos theory, the inevitable pint of *Guinness*.

Special effects and dazzling sets were increasingly employed to cover up the cracks that were beginning to appear in the underlying idea. In 1994 Hauer made his last appearance in a *Guinness* commercial, relegated to a flickering image in a television screen in the commercial "Chain". This commercial extended the idea of a swirling journey through a glass of *Guinness* and back out again and was set to two different soundtracks, one featuring frenetic rock music by the British band Slaughterhouse, the second a wonderfully relaxing rendition of "All the Time in the World" by Louis Armstrong. □

Poster 1992

Agency Ogilvy & Mather

Ogilvy & Mather's "Fractionals" campaign was versatile enough to be used in a variety of different media from newspapers to bus shelters. The simplistic black-and-white doodles were intended to appear as the causal jottings of "The Man with the Guinness".

Press advertisement 1995

Agency Ogilvy & Mather

The simplicity of the "Fractionals" campaign meant that topical advertisements could be turned around quickly and efficiently.

Press advertisement 1995

Agency Ogilvy & Mather

The sports pages of the national newspapers provided an effective backdrop for many advertisements in the "Fractionals" campaign.

Poster 1991

Agency Ogilvy & Mather

This was a lateral take on *Guinness'* highly distinctive colour scheme.

Poster 1992

Agency Ogilvy & Mather

The backgrounds into which the glasses of *Guinness* were dropped provided the key to the campaign's humour.

Poster 1992

Agency Ogilvy & Mather

Occasionally, the voice of "The Man with the Guinness" pushed through in the "Fractionals" campaign.

Poster 1992

Agency Ogilvy & Mather

In this "Fractional", an on-going dialogue was established with the audience.

Press advertisement 1994

Agency Ogilvy & Mather

This visual inversion recalled the "Australian for Genius" poster.

Poster 1992

Agency Ogilvy & Mather

Once the essential visual
framework had been
established, it could easily be
subverted and toyed with.

**Press advertisement
1995**

Agency Ogivly & Mather

Here a pint of *Guinness*
was given a sharp
seasonal twist.

Press advertisement 1994

Agency Ogilvy & Mather

This was an extremely
rare foray into colour for
the "Fractionals" print
campaign.

Press advertisement 1992

Agency Ogilvy & Mather

The "Fractionals" campaign, originally developed
as the doodlings of "The Man with the Guinness",
quickly developed an identity of its own.

Irish advertising

In the early 1950s, when Guinness began tentatively placing advertising on city bus routes in Dublin, a local man memorably told *Time* magazine that, "Advertising Guinness is like advertising potatoes". He had a point. *Guinness* stout has been brewed in Dublin since the late 18th Century and is an established Irish institution. The souvenir shop in Dublin Airport is a testament to how integral *Guinness* has become to the Irish heritage industry; there is more *Guinness* paraphernalia on display than shamrocks, harps and lucky leprechauns put together.

On one level, there seemed little point in advertising *Guinness* in Ireland; everyone knew about it anyway and fully appreciated its finer points. From the 1930s to the late 1950s, Guinness spent a mere £10,000 per annum on advertising, taking small spaces in programmes for community and sporting events, producing *Guinness* playing cards and sometimes bringing pub showcards over from England. But circumstances changed in the late 1950s, when *Guinness'* supremacy was threatened by emerging competition in the form of imported beer brands arriving from Britain.

The first Irish *Guinness* campaign appeared in 1959, to celebrate the brewery's bicentenary. The slogan was by Stanley Penn, one of Bensons' most accomplished copy-writers, and it read: "200 years of Guinness. What a lovely long drink". Bensons continued to ship over suitable posters as and when appropriate, while Arks, a Dublin-based agency, took charge of media buying and offered advice on the local market. Radio Telefis Eireann (RTE), the Irish television service, was launched in 1961, and though Guinness quickly established itself as a major advertiser, its early commercials, which attempted pub humour, had little impact.

Arks took full control of *Guinness* advertising in Ireland in 1969, at the same time as JWT inherited the account from Bensons in Britain. Its first campaign, "There's more than goodness in Guinness", played on the original "Guinness is good for you" slogan, showing glasses and bottles of *Guinness* in a selection of environments, and

Poster 1970

Agency Arks

This was part of Arks' first campaign, "There's more than goodness in Guinness".

Poster 1971

Agency Arks

The "More than goodness..." campaign played on the ending of the word "Guinness"

Poster 1971

Agency Arks

Wordplay loomed large in another of Arks' early posters for *Guinness* in Ireland.

SOMETIMES WE FEEL THE WHOLE WORLD IS AGUINNESS

It is. So it isn't.

endowing them with an appropriate "-ness". For example, a domestic scene was captioned "Homeliness"; a *Guinness* outside in some lush grass surrounded by fresh fruit, "Summerness"; a pub table weighed down by pints of *Guinness*, "Guinnessness".

A carefully composed photographic poster from 1976, "Ireland's great natural resource", showed a pint of *Guinness* next to a detailed map of the west coast of the island along with photographs of oil platforms, a compass and a ruler. In 1982, a pair of bright red lips poised to take a sip from a glass of *Guinness* (reminiscent of J Walter Thompson's "Ladylike", page 116) ushered in the "No beer comes near" campaign, which went on to feature a string of mainly Irish celebrities, including the folk group The Chieftains and Clannad, and footballers Frank Stapleton, Mark Lawrenson and Ray Houghton.

In terms of television work, Arks' highlights included the 1977 commercial "Island", which won several international awards, including a Silver Lion at the blue-riband Cannes International Advertising Festival and a highly prestigious Clio in New York. Directed by John Devis, this featured a rural bar crowded with people, yet totally silent. The only sound to be heard is the ticking of a clock. The film cuts to a traditional Irish 'currach' slowly making its way to the shore. The rowers get out and begin to carry a keg of *Guinness* up a cliff path towards the pub. They enter and deliver the beer in silence.

The publican pours the beer and the crowd comes to life, everyone excitedly talking in Irish. The closing caption is also in Irish.

"Surfer" (1980), also known as "Big Wave", first appeared as a 48-sheet poster, but was transformed into a spectacular two-minute television and cinema commercial (cut-down versions were also used). It showed a surfer apparently riding the crest of a huge wave of *Guinness*. " 'Surfer' changed the face of Guinness advertising in Ireland," claims Trevor Jacobs, a director of Arks. "It made it far more contemporary. The commercial was like a Rorschach ink-blot test. People projected their own feelings and emotions on to it."

A more recent Arks success story was "Anticipation" from 1994, which showed a *Guinness* drinker, played by Irish actor Joe McKinney, dancing maniacally around a pint of Guinness as he waits for it to settle. The exaggerated perspectives – with the *Guinness* centre stage and McKinney inspecting it impatiently from all angles – and the manic music, "Guaglione", by the Perez Prado Orchestra, complemented the crazy dancing perfectly. Joe McKinney became a minor celebrity, Perez Prado entered the music charts, and public awareness of the commercial ran at 85 per cent. In 1995, in the lull between Ogilvy & Mather's "The Man with the Guinness" and "Black and White" campaigns, "Anticipation" was aired on British television, and achieved instant cult status.

Poster 1971

Agency Arks

This was an Irish precursor of Ogilvy & Mather's "Genius" campaign.

Poster 1980

Agency Arks

"Surfer", also known as "Big Wave", was a poster that inspired a famous television and cinema commercial, which changed the face of *Guinness* advertising in Ireland.

Poster 1973

Agency Arks

This was part of the "Get together with a Guinness" campaign, which associated *Guinness* with song and sociability.

Poster 1976

Agency Arks

A sepia-toned, romanticised view of Ireland emerged in a women's poster campaign.

Arks' advertising embraced a range of styles in its "Get together with a Guinness", "At home with a Guinness" and "Have a Guinness Tonight" campaigns. In its latter years, it concentrated on projecting a more stylish, contemporary flavour, shifting *Guinness'* emphasis towards the younger drinker and away from its traditional rural Irish image.

In 1996, the advertising agency Bell produced a "Black and White" campaign, in a similar vein to that used in Britain, but using different quotations. This was replaced later in the same year by the "Big Pint" campaign, devised by the London-based agency Howell, Henry, Chaldecott, Lury &

Partners, which in Britain is best-known for its work on Tango and the AA. The campaign brought the focus of the advertising firmly back to the product itself; in terms of taste, depth, creaminess, and drinking experience, *Guinness* can justifiably be described as a "big" pint, and this notion informed the entire campaign. "We wanted to emphasise the power of the pint, its largeness and its gulpabilty," explains John Leach, a planner at Howell, Henry, Chaldecott, Lury & Partners.

Posters showed a pint of *Guinness* photographed slightly from below, lending an exaggerated perspective to the glass; they appear almost to be bulging out of the

Poster 1978

Agency Arks

This Arks poster is highly reminiscent of J Walter Thompson's work. The photograph was subsequently used on the front cover of a Guinness annual report.

Press advertisement 1981

Agency Arks

Used mostly in women's magazines, this advertisement quashed the myth that *Guinness* is highly calorific.

poster. Bold, bald captions are placed next to the shot of the pint, they read: "XXXL", "4D" and "The mother of all pints". Positioned at the baggage collection point at Dublin Airport and on the main road to the city centre, a poster reads, "Welcome to the home of the world's biggest pint", a reference not only to the fact that Dublin is the home of the world's biggest selling pint, but also that more pints of *Guinness* are consumed worldwide than any other beer.

Humorous television commercials featured men of various nationalities pondering how a big pint could fit into a human hand. A follow-up commercial introducing a larger sized Draught *Guinness*

in a can showed items of furniture being thrown from a first-floor window. "I need more space!" come the desperate cries from within. Further Howell, Henry, Chaldecott, Lury & Partners campaigns stressed refreshment and targeted younger drinkers.

Clearly, British and Irish audiences have totally different perceptions of *Guinness* and the advertising should recognise and reflect the respective starting points. "Guinness is *the* national drink," insists Trevor Jacobs. "When Arks took over the account it outsold all the other beers in Ireland put together, so one of the main objectives of Guinness advertising in Ireland has always been to reassure existing drinkers."

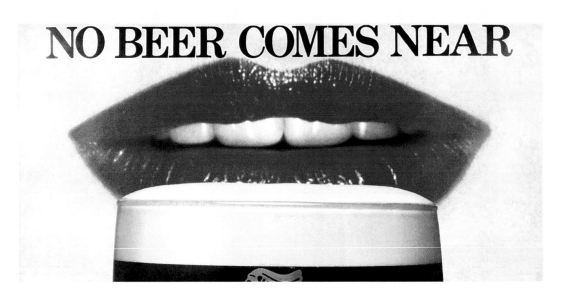

Poster 1982

Agency Arks

This was the first poster in the "No beer comes near" campaign, which introduced the line.

Poster 1983

Agency Arks

Subsequent posters used personalites including The Chieftains (above), Clannad, Mike Oldfield and several soccer players.

Press advertisement 1990

Agency Arks

This topical advertisement ran during the 1990
World Cup, when Ireland was due to play Italy.

Poster 1991

Agency Arks

This ran in tandem with another poster with
the words "Cool, calm and collect it", in which
the third beer was still in place.

Poster 1991

Agency Arks

Unusually, the *Guinness* harp was the starting point for a creative idea.

Poster 1993

Agency Arks

The "Cool" campaign ran every summer in Ireland for many years, boosted by television and radio spots.

Poster 1994

Agency Arks

The "Anticipation" posters were a spin-off from the highly popular commercial.

Poster 1994

Agency Arks

The "Guinness time" slogan harked back to the early days of SH Benson.

Poster 1994

Agency Arks

"Dancing" Joe McKinney built up a cult following in Ireland.

Poster 1996

Agency Howell, Henry, Chaldecott, Lury & Partners

This double meaning was either a reference to *Guinness'* lengthy history or to its "bigness".

Poster 1996

Agency Howell, Henry, Chaldecott, Lury & Partners

This poster was positioned on the main road to the city centre from Dublin Airport.

Poster 1996

Agency Howell, Henry,
Chaldecott, Lury & Partners

The pint of *Guinness* is
photographed slightly
from below to emphasise
its size and fullness.

Poster 1996

Agency Howell, Henry,
Chaldecott, Lury & Partners

Curiously, there is a sense
of the pint glass emerging
from the poster, as if it
were a 3-D object.

Poster 1997

Agency Howell, Henry, Chaldecott, Lury & Partners

This was part of an Irish summer campaign emphasising refreshment, but stressing *Guinness'* point of difference from lagers.

Poster 1997

Agency Howell, Henry, Chaldecott, Lury & Partners

The idea may be reminiscent of "Surfer", but the graphic style is harder and more contemporary.

Poster 1997
Agency Howell, Henry, Chaldecott, Lury &
Partners
Artist M Bartalos

Summer posters were aimed at attracting the younger *Guinness* drinker. San Franciscan illustrator Michael Bartalos brought a quirky style to the campaign.

Black and White

During the early part of the 1990s, advertisers detected a distinct shift in

consumer values and attitudes. The 1980s' accent on materialism and

individualism was fading fast and being replaced by a less superficial,

more considered mood. Consumers sought authenticity in the brands they

favoured; their choices came to signify a personal appreciation of a brand's

values and complexities rather than acting as a symbol of their wealth or

status. Substance was in. Veneer was out.

Poster 1996

Agency Ogilvy & Mather

The self-referential tone in this poster was typical of the pervasive post-modern sensibility.

Poster 1996

Agency Ogilvy & Mather

The ironic self-mockery of the copy included the cryptic twist expected of *Guinness* advertising.

As a result of economic recession, people had become even more disillusioned with the future. Culturally, there was an upsurge in post-modernism as a tongue-in-cheek self-consciousness pervaded the worlds of art, fashion and music. Nothing, apparently, could be taken at face value any more. If you looked hard enough, there was always a joke, parody or a statement lurking behind the façade.

In this context, the tone and demeanour of "The Man with the Guinness" had begun to appear a bit smug. Here was someone who was too clever for his own good. He had all the answers, yet the prevailing climate seemed to be more about questions than answers. Recent history, the civil war in former Yugoslavia in particular, had demonstrated that there were no cut-and-dried answers. As a slogan, "Pure Genius" seemed out of step with the times. It was little too sure of itself in an uncertain world where nothing was black-and-white.

On top of this, *Guinness'* advertising was no longer unique, the format of "The Man with the Guinness" commercials having been widely imitated by rival beer brands. Furthermore there was Murphy's, the first of a batch of Irish stouts now available on the British market. When poured, many of these beers looked exactly like *Guinness*; the black pint with a creamy white head was no longer the distinctive "logo in a glass" it once had been. The time was ripe for a new advertising offensive to reaffirm Guinness' position in an increasingly crowded and competitive beer sector.

The result was Ogilvy & Mather's "Black and White" campaign, conceived by the art director Clive Yaxley and copywriter Jerry Gallagher. It was launched in February 1996 with a pair of "teaser" posters. They were stark and distinctive, using the jagged Bell

Gothic typeface in white, reversed out of a black background, and styled by talented and controversial typographer Jonathan Barnbrook. "It was designed to be as clean and contrasty as possible," says Yaxley.

Each poster consisted of a single attributed quotation: "Hope I die before I get old" (Pete Townshend) – taken from The Who's Mod anthem, "My Generation" – and "A woman needs a man like a fish needs a bicycle" (graffiti). The words were typeset in contrasting sizes, and some were framed for emphasis. The overall effect was raw, contemporary and intriguing.

In March, two television commercials, featuring the same quotations, were released. They were both shot by Tony Kaye, one of the most colourful commercials directors working in the advertising industry. The strength of Kaye's advertising films lies in their visual impact; recent examples include "Twister" for Volvo through the advertising agency Abbott Mead Vickers BBDO, which involved creating a tornado using powerful aircraft engines, and Dunlop tyres' "Tested for the Unexpected" commercial through the same agency, a surreal journey through a nightmare landscape inhabited by malevolent sprites.

The first of Kaye's pair of *Guinness* commercials, "Old Man", featured a pensioner at home with his budgie, goldfish and false teeth in a jar. It is artfully shot in black-and-white and, appropriately enough, cut to the soundtrack "My Generation" by The Who. He is shown slowly and methodically getting himself dressed for a wedding and feeding his pets. The Townshend quotation flashes across the screen; then the scene shifts to the steps of a registry office. The old man is pictured arm-in-arm with his new wife, a heavily pregnant blonde, who can't be much more than a quarter of his age.

"YOU'VE MORE CHANCE OF SEEING A LEPRECHAUN THAN ME WITH A GUINNESS ON ST. PAT'S"

GEORGE BEST

ON MARCH 17TH

NOT EVERYTHING IN BLACK AND WHITE MAKES SENSE

Posters 1996
Agency Ogilvy & Mather

The "Black and White"
campaign adopted a topical
slant for St Patrick's Day.

The second commercial, "Bicycle", opens with a group of women drinking in a bar. Flashbacks show these women at work doing jobs traditionally associated with men: mining, drilling roads and driving lorries. The quote "A woman needs a man like a fish needs a bicycle" appears, followed by a shot of an empty maternity ward. Both these two commercials conclude with the sign-off: "Not everything in black and white makes sense."

Both advertisements neatly subverted the viewer's expectations and sparked off the desired level of debate. They reaffirmed *Guinness* as a surprising, challenging drink supported by cutting-edge advertising. In August 1996, twelve more posters, conceived by the creative team Adam Denton and Andy Fairless, were launched using provocative quotations presented in a similar graphic style. By this time, campaign awareness was running at 53 per cent. → p. 230

Poster 1997

Agency Ogilvy & Mather

Image and quotation combined to achieve an arresting effect.

Poster 1997

Agency Ogilvy & Mather

The "Black and White" campaign was intended to be provocative.

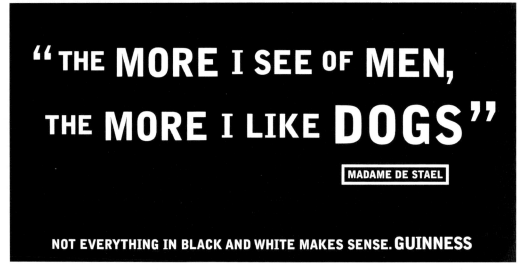

Poster 1996

Agency Ogilvy & Mather

This implied *Guinness* was a good taste worth acquiring.

Poster 1996

Agency Ogilvy & Mather

Typographic styling by Jonathan Barnbrook gave an added visual dimension.

Press advertisements 1997

Agency Ogilvy & Mather

These advertisements were tailored for
the sports pages of the nationals.

Two more commercials in the "Black and White" series appeared during 1997. "Fishing" used unsettling juxtapositions of images: a crowded seaside scene and a multitude of golfers using a driving range which cuts to a mass of writhing maggots. These examples of frenetic activity were contrasted with a tranquil fishing scene and the quotation, "Fishing is complete and utter madness" (Spike Milligan).

The final commercial, shot by the commercials director Chris Palmer, was called "Statistics" and launched in May 1997. More humorous and accessible than the earlier advertisements in the campaign, it runs through a series of spurious but plausible statistics,

marrying them with appropriate images. They include: "The average cow passes enough wind in a week to inflate a hot air balloon" (a hot air balloon in the shape of a cow) and "36 per cent of strippers had a convent education" (a stripper). The concluding quotation reads, "88.2 per cent of statistics are made up on the spot" (Vic Reeves). "Statistics" proved particularly adaptable to below-the-line efforts, with mind-boggling facts and figures making their way on to bar mats in pubs to encourage further discussion of contentious claims.

Like Gilroy's work some 70 years earlier Ogilvy & Mather's "Black and White" campaign was a potent

▸ p. 237

"IF WOMEN DRESSED FOR MEN, STORES WOULDN'T SELL MUCH, JUST THE OCCASIONAL SUN VISOR"

GROUCHO MARX

NOT EVERYTHING IN BLACK AND WHITE MAKES SENSE. GUINNESS

Press advertisement 1996

Agency Ogilvy & Mather

The Bell Gothic typeface is easily recognisable by the serif on the letter "I".

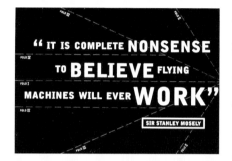

" IT IS COMPLETE NONSENSE TO BELIEVE FLYING MACHINES WILL EVER WORK"

SIR STANLEY MOSELY

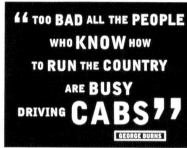

" TOO BAD ALL THE PEOPLE WHO KNOW HOW TO RUN THE COUNTRY ARE BUSY DRIVING CABS"

GEORGE BURNS

LICENCED **LONDON TAXI** RECEIPT

FARE £

DATE

SIGNATURE

NOT EVERYTHING IN BLACK AND WHITE MAKES SENSE. GUINNESS

Postcard 1997

Agency Ogilvy & Mather

Below-the-line efforts have been used to support the main thrust of the campaign.

Cab receipt (front and back) 1997

Agency Ogilvy & Mather

This is an example of so-called "guerrilla" advertising.

" SERVE **CHILLED**"

THE CAN

NOT EVERYTHING IN BLACK AND WHITE MAKES SENSE

Poster 1997

Agency BRANN

Here the "Black and White" approach encourages sales for cold Draught *Guinness* in cans as part of a poster and radio campaign.

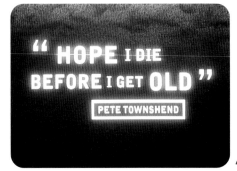

Commercial 1996

Agency Ogilvy & Mather
Director T Kaye

"Old Man" was the first of four "Black and White" commercials to be aired. It subverted the viewer's expectations by depicting an old man in shabby domestic surroundings. It later transpired he was getting ready to marry a young, glamorous – and heavily pregnant – blonde woman. The message is clear: you can't judge entirely by appearances.

"A WOMAN NEEDS A MAN LIKE A FISH NEEDS A BICYCLE"

GRAFFITI

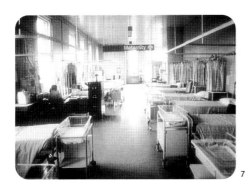

Commercial 1996

Agency Ogilvy & Mather
Director T Kaye

In the second
commercial, women
were shown at work in
jobs traditionally
associated with men.
The fish on the bicycle (8)
was transformed into
a highly acclaimed
PC screen-saver.

Commercial 1997
Agency Ogilvy & Mather
Director T Kaye

The third commercial in the series contrasted noisy, overcrowded holiday and leisure scenes with the serenity of a day's fishing on the river bank.

7

8

9

10

11

Several consecutive mirror images introduced a rich chiaroscuro, emphasising the visual contrast inherent in *Guinness* itself and the underlying motif of the "Black and White" campaign. The white slogan is placed over a pint of *Guinness* which becomes clearer as the drink settles into a deep, rich black colour.

"The average cow passes enough wind in a week to inflate a hot-air balloon."

"88 per cent of clowns never fall in love."

"36 per cent of strippers had a convent education."

"Every year over 300 animals escape from zoos and circuses."

"98 per cent of Man United fans have never been to Old Trafford."

7

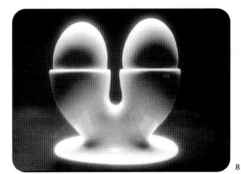

8

"Men think about sex every six seconds."

Commercial 1997
Agency Ogilvy & Mather
Director C Palmer

"Statistics", directed by Chris Palmer, was more light-hearted than the previous three commercials. Based around a quote attributed to the British comedian Vic Reeves ("88.2 per cent of statistics are made up on the spot"), it ran through a number of dubious facts and figures, accompanied by a series of bizarre visual tableaux designed to illustrate them.

9

The penultimate quasi-subliminal frame of "Statistics".

encapsulation of the spirit of the age. The best advertising tends to reflect, and to an extent define, the stylistic and cultural preoccupations of an era; the "Black and White" campaign's deliberately raw, knowing aesthetic, together with its exploration of the tangled moral maze contemporary living, struck a chord with media-literate mid-1990s drinkers. It had attitude without being threatening; it was cryptic and occasionally uncomfortable, yet still compelling and comprehensible. By March 1997 *Guinness* had achieved its highest ever share of the total British beer market at 5.2 per cent.

The challenge facing any modern-day *Guinness* campaign is to speak in a relevant, topical voice, but at the same time to respect both the outstanding

advertising heritage and carefully nurtured brand equity of the product. It's a tall order and comparisons are inevitable; the *Guinness* drinker and the consumer of *Guinness* advertising have come to expect the extraordinary. Lateral ideas and incisive, original wit aren't enough by themselves, visual styling and production values have to be of the highest order too.

It's a daunting task, but it's also a unique opportunity; one that every major advertising agency would relish. After all, the gems have been numerous, and as *Guinness* advertising in Britain enters the next phase of its eventful history under the auspices of Abbott Mead Vickers BBDO, it looks set to maintain *Guinness'* position as the century's pre-eminent brand. □

Acknowledgements

The author wishes to thank the following for consultation and assistance in the making of this book:

David Abbott, Jane Austin, Jon Barnbrook, Martin Borrett, Tom Bury, Sue Garland, John Gilroy, Trevor Jacobs, Deborah Kings, Mari Takayanagi, John Wheelhouse, Chris Wilkins.

Guinness Publishing would like to give special thanks to Sue Garland at Guinness Archives for all her help in putting the book together.

Thanks are also due to the following: Steve Day, Paul Gilham, Marcus Husselby, Trevor Jacobs, Anna Morgan.

Guinness Archives gratefully acknowledges the contribution that the Ian Livingstone Collection has made to their collection.

Photographic Acknowledgements

p 143– 149 all photographic stills courtesy BFI stills, posters and designs; p 170–173 all photographic stills courtesy Jim Davies; p 189 (bottom picture), p 192, p 193, p 194, p 195, p 196, p 197 all reproduced by kind permission of Rutger Hauer.

All other photographs © Guinness Limited

Bibliography

Barnicoat, John. *Posters: a Concise History*. Thames & Hudson, 1988.

Begley, George. *Keep Mum! Advertising Goes to War*. Lemon Tree Press, 1975.

Bernstein, David. *Watch This Space: Advertising Outdoors*. Phaidon, 1997.

Dichter, Ernest. *The Strategy of Desire*. Doubleday, 1960.

Dobrow, Larry. *When Advertising Tried Harder. The Sixties: The Golden Age of American Advertising*. Friendly Press, 1984.

Douglas, Torin. *The Complete Guide to Advertising*. Macmillan, 1984

Guinness, Edward. *Guinness Book of Guinness*. Guinness Publishing, 1988.

Heller, Steven and Chwast, Seymour. *Graphic Style: From Victorian to Post-Modern*. Thames and Hudson, 1988.

Heller, Steven and Anderson, Gail. *Graphic Wit: The Art of Humour in Design*. Watson-Guptill, 1991.

Henry, Brian (ed). *British Television Advertising, The First 30 Years*. Century Benham, 1986.

Holme, Bryan. *The Art of Advertising*. Peerage Books, 1982.

Ind, Nicholas. *Great Advertising Campaigns*. Kogan Page, 1993.

McLuhan, Eric and Zingrone, Frank, eds. *Essential McLuhan*. Routledge, 1997.

Meggs, Philip B. *A History of Graphic Design*. Van Nostrand Reinhold Company, 1983.

Morris Rob and Watson Richard. *The World's 100 Best Posters*. Open Eye, 1993.

Myers, William. *The Image Makers*. Time Books, 1984.

Nevett, TR. *Advertising in Britain: A History*. Heinemann, 1982

Packard, Vance. *The Hidden Persuaders*. Longmans Green, 1957.

Price, Jonathan. *The Best Thing on TV: Commercials*. Penguin, 1978.

Souter, Nick and Newman, Stuart. *The Creative Director's Sourcebook*. Macdonald Orbis, 1988.

Treasure, Dr JAP. *The History of British Advertising Agencies 1875-1939*. Scottish Academic Press, 1977.

Articles:
"Guinness is good". *Direction magazine*, November 1987

"Advertising: the Mother of Graphic Design". *Eye magazine* No 17, Volume 5.

"AMV Guinness win seals position as dominant agency". *Campaign*, 16 January 1998.

"Guinness the O&M years". *Campaign*. 23 January 1998.